R-2868-NIE

Federal Influence Over State and Local Government: The Case of Nondiscrimination in Education

Paul T. Hill and Ellen L. Marks

December 1982

Prepared for the
National Institute of Education

SANTA MONICA, CA. 90406

PREFACE

This report is based on research supported by a grant from the National Institute of Education's Legal and Governmental Studies Program. The study examined strategies used by the government to influence state and local educational policy. Its purpose was to clarify how different influence methods work and to identify the circumstances under which each is most and least effective.

The primary audience for this report consists of federal policymakers, both the members of Congress who establish societal goals and allocate resources to programs, and officials of the Executive Branch who decide how and when program resources are used. A second audience comprises interested parties, particularly the associations of state and local public service officials and Washington-based interest groups that represent program beneficiaries. A third audience includes academic students of intergovernmental relations who may see the findings as steps toward a general theory of federal influence.

SUMMARY

This is a study of the federal government's efforts to influence state and local governments. It focuses on education--on how two divisions of the U.S. Department of Education try to influence states and local school districts, and how the latter respond. But we propose that the results apply not only to education but to many areas in which the federal government tries to change the policies of states and localities.

The study examines the Department of Education's Office for Civil Rights (OCR) and the Office of Special Education (OSE). OCR is responsible for administering laws that prohibit discrimination on the basis of race, sex, national origin, or handicap in federally funded education programs. OCR conducts compliance reviews, responds to citizen complaints, and penalizes states and localities that violate civil rights laws. OSE administers PL 94-142, which provides approximately $1 billion in annual grants to states and school districts to provide a "free appropriate public education" to all handicapped children. OSE uses a multifaceted grants program designed to improve local efforts on behalf of the handicapped.

The two agencies have similar goals--changing state and local policies toward disadvantaged students--but they use very different methods. By comparing OCR's and OSE's methods and results, we identify different kinds of leverage available to federal agencies, and frame general statements about how effective each source of leverage is in changing state and local policy.

Our data come from exhaustive case studies of OCR and OSE. We examined their staffing patterns, staff beliefs and orientations toward their jobs, general policies and procedures for dealing with states and localities, and their actual conduct in meeting and negotiating with state and local officials. We used these data to compare the agencies' operating styles and assumptions, methods of influence, and effects on state and local agencies.

OPERATING STYLES AND ASSUMPTIONS

OCR and OSE have very different images of themselves and the state and local officials they try to influence. OCR sees itself as a prosecutor: Its job is to identify violations of the law and either punish violators or use the threat of punishment as leverage to obtain compliance. OSE sees itself as a facilitator of voluntary local efforts: Its job is to put resources into the hands of local professionals and beneficiary groups to improve services for the handicapped. OCR employees generally work under the assumption that local decisionmaking processes are biased against disadvantaged groups, and that federal intervention is necessary to protect civil rights. OSE staff generally assume that local officials are friendly to the interests of the handicapped, and that local beneficiary groups, especially the parents of handicapped children, can effectively assert their own interests.

These differences are clearly rooted in the two agencies' histories: OCR's first task was to supervise the desegregation of southern schools, while OSE's first task was to administer a program of practitioner-initiated research and development grants. The two agencies have maintained their original orientations despite important changes in the scope and content of their portfolios.

INFLUENCE METHODS

Each agency has developed several methods for influencing state and local policy (see Table S.1). Though their overall repertoires of influence methods are very similar, their emphases differ markedly.

Table S.2 shows how the two agencies differ in their use of the available influence methods. Three important differences are apparent. First, OSE uses a broader range of influence mechanisms than does OCR. Second, OCR relies primarily on mechanisms that require direct federal involvement in monitoring local activities and imposing costs and penalties. Third, in contrast, OSE's primary methods rely on the self-interested actions of local individuals, particularly special education professionals and parents of handicapped children. These differences reflect the two organizations' distinct histories, philosophies, and

Table S.1

INFLUENCE METHODS AVAILABLE TO OCR AND OSE

Threat of corporate penalties: threatened decreases in the local agency's income through imposition of fines or withholding of future grants.

Individual sanctions: increases in personal stress or potential damage to the careers or incomes of local officials who must respond to federal enforcement or local complaints by beneficiaries.

Process costs: imposition of demands for expenditure of time and money to keep records, make reports, cooperate with federal monitoring, rebut charges, appeal the imposition of penalties, or respond to demands by beneficiaries.

Corporate rewards: increases in local agencies' income through discretionary grants or prizes.[a]

Individual rewards: increases in incomes, satisfaction, reputations, or career prospects of local officials who promote local compliance with federal requirements.

Technical assistance: help in implementing policy changes required by regulation by providing expert advice, staff training, self-assessment manuals, and models of compliant local programs.

Encouraging beneficiary organizations: helping beneficiary groups to organize at the national, state, and local levels by providing subsidies to such groups or requiring state and local governments to establish them.

Creating leverage for beneficiaries and advocates: establishment of specific beneficiary rights to obtain information about, be consulted about, approve, or contest local policy decisions.

---

[a]The typology excludes formula grants because they can be created only by Congressional statutes and appropriations, and are therefore not given at the discretion of federal agencies.

resulting broad strategies: the first strategy, reflecting OCR's dominant mode of influence, we call enforcement; the second, reflecting OSE's emphasis, we call promotion.

EFFECTS ON STATE AND LOCAL AGENCIES

To assess the effects of the strategies, we sought evidence about whether contacts with OSE or OCR had changed school districts in either of two ways: first, by making their decisionmaking procedures more open and responsive to federal program goals; and second, by changing their policies and procedures on behalf of federal program beneficiaries.

We found that both OCR's enforcement and OSE's promotional activity strongly affected school districts' decisionmaking processes. Districts uniformly found their first encounters with OCR investigators very stressful, but in subsequent encounters most had established clear bureaucratic procedures for negotiating with OCR and implementing compliance agreements.

OSE does not investigate school districts or negotiate with them directly, but it does promote the establishment of formal due process systems for the resolution of complaints initiated by handicapped children or their parents. The first complaint handled through any district's system is usually treated as a crisis; after the first one or

Table S.2

COMPARISON OF OCR'S AND OSE'S USE OF INFLUENCE METHODS

Method	Importance of Method	
	OCR	OSE
Threat of corporate penalties	Secondary	Slight
Individual sanctions	Secondary	Slight
Process costs	Primary	Slight
Corporate rewards	Slight	Secondary
Individual rewards	Slight	Primary
Technical assistance	Slight	Primary
Beneficiary organizations	Slight	Primary
Beneficiary leverage	Slight	Primary

two cases are settled, however, complaint processing becomes routinized and district officials learn how to resolve individual cases without making major changes in district policy.

Our findings about the substantive results of OCR's enforcement efforts can be summarized as follows:

o   OCR investigations, negotiations, and sanctions definitely can produce change at the local level.

o   The changes produced are limited in scope. Enforcement can: (1) produce a specific adjustment in a service; (2) change the local agency's treatment of a particular individual or a small, easily identifiable group; or (3) produce a change in administrative practices. But it seldom affects the overall distribution of services within a district or the school district's general orientation to all members of a disadvantaged group.

o   Local educational agencies apparently make the changes that they expressly and unambiguously promise, but take advantage of any ambiguities in their agreement with OCR.

It is very difficult to compare the substantive results of enforcement with the outcomes obtained through promotion because promotion affects district policy indirectly. Nonetheless, it is clear that OSE's promotional activities have contributed to important changes in local policy, including:

o   Increases in special education's share of the total education budget. Local interest groups, encouraged by OSE and buttressed by PL 94-142, have effectively lobbied school boards and state legislatures for budget increases.

o   Quick adoption of new special education practices. OSE's technical assistance programs ensure that local staff and parents learn quickly about new therapies and instructional techniques.

o   Implementation of new legal doctrines. OSE disseminates the
     results of landmark court cases that expand the range of
     services to which handicapped children are entitled.

Comparing the results of OCR's and OSE's efforts makes promotion
look like the more effective strategy. There is, however, reason to
think that federal goals in special education had far more local support
and were, therefore, much easier to accomplish than the goals of OCR's
programs. To form a valid picture of the comparative strengths and
weaknesses of enforcement and promotion, we tried to identify the
circumstances under which each is likely to be most and least effective.

CAPACITIES AND LIMITS OF FEDERAL INFLUENCE STRATEGIES

Section V of the report applies our findings about OCR and OSE to
general questions about the federal government's capacities and
limitations in dealing with state and local governments. The section
establishes a general framework for choosing federal influence
strategies and anticipating their likely effects. The framework has
three elements: the barriers that federal influence efforts might need
to overcome; the strategies by which the federal government can try to
overcome the barriers; and the costs that the use of particular
strategies imposes on the federal government.

Barriers

The essential common purpose of federal domestic programs is to
help or induce states, localities, and firms to do things that they
would not or could not do if left on their own. Federal policies and
programs are, therefore, meant to overcome any barriers to the
attainment of national goals. The possible barriers fit into five
categories: (1) technical intractability--the absence of the materials,
machinery, or skills required to attain a goal; (2) lack of support--
unwillingness on the part of state or local officeholders, service
providers, or citizens to make the necessary changes; (3) opposition--
resistance to the necessary changes from state or local officeholders,
service providers, or citizens; (4) lack of knowledge--local

unfamiliarity with procedures or mechanisms to implement the necessary changes; and (5) insufficient resources--the absence of funds required to pay for the necessary changes.

Strategies

The available strategies include the two most used by OCR and OSE--enforcement and promotion--and one other, subsidy. Subsidy involves paying state and local governments to change their policies: The federal government provides funds to offset the costs of desired changes.

Costs

All of the influence strategies in our framework impose costs on the federal government.

The costs of subsidy are financial. It involves direct transfers of federal funds to state or local governments to pay for desired changes. In theory, subsidies enable local governments to provide new services thought desirable by the federal government at no cost to themselves.

The costs of promotion are measured in federal funds for developing professions dedicated to program purposes, providing technical assistance to improve local expertise for service delivery, and helping local groups to organize and to gain access to local decisionmaking processes. These costs are generally far less than the costs of subsidy.

The costs of enforcement are political. Political costs arise whenever a government action hurts or offends a politically powerful person or group. In general, the political costs of a governmental action are a function of the opposition that action stimulates.

When establishing a new program, the government can make some choices about the kinds of costs it wants to pay. Other things being equal, the federal government pays smaller political costs for a program that emphasizes cash subsidies; conversely, the government can accept political costs in lieu of providing subsidies by strongly enforcing a requirement.

Implications

There are some obvious logical matches between barriers and strategies. Subsidy is the obvious way to overcome the lack of local resources; enforcement overcomes local opposition by making noncompliance more costly than compliance; promotion overcomes any weakness in local support for federal program goals by strengthening the hands of beneficiary groups and allied service providers.

In general, there are strict limits to the substitution of one influence strategy for another. Use of the wrong influence method can impose enormous costs to no effect. Enforcement, no matter how aggressive and politically costly it is, cannot work if a goal is technically intractable or if local officials lack the skills to make necessary changes in services. Subsidy, no matter how great, cannot overcome lack of knowledge. Likewise, promotion, no matter how comprehensive and skillfully done, cannot overcome total local opposition or lack of funds.

Many federal goals face multiple barriers, and thus require hybrid strategies that mix elements of subsidy, enforcement, and promotion. To facilitate the construction of hybrid strategies, we trace the logical connections between all possible combinations of barriers and the mixtures of strategies necessary to overcome them.

Four general propositions suggest how the federal government should select influence strategies to achieve particular goals:

1. The effectiveness of federal influence efforts depends on establishing the correct match between federal program goals and local conditions. For each federal program there is a particular combination of local support, knowledge, and available resources; a strategy tailored to match that set of circumstances will be the most effective.

2. Conversely, the failure to establish the correct match between federal goals and local conditions creates ineffective and needlessly costly programs. Poorly selected strategies can create large financial and political costs and destroy the federal government's reputation for competence.

3. Local circumstances also determine the kinds and amounts of
    costs that the federal government must pay to attain any goal.
    The federal government must pay different kinds of costs to
    overcome lack of local support, knowledge, or fiscal resources.
    The level of any one cost depends on the degree to which local
    conditions must be changed. Though it is possible to shift
    some costs from one form to another, the least-cost strategy is
    usually the one that most directly addresses the local
    circumstances.

4. No one influence strategy is always the best for all goals or
    circumstances. The best strategy to achieve a goal may differ
    from time to time and from place to place, and many goals may
    require complex hybrid strategies. The fact that a strategy
    worked well for one goal or in one class of jurisdiction does
    not mean that it will work well for others.

ACKNOWLEDGMENTS

This report has benefited from the contributions of many people. We wish to thank Donald W. Burnes, David Goodwin, and Grace Mastalli at the National Institute of Education for providing background data, factual information, and comments on the draft report.

Our reviewers for this study were George C. Eads of Rand and the University of Maryland, and Frank J. Sorauf of the University of Minnesota. Linda Darling-Hammond of Rand offered many helpful suggestions throughout the course of this study. We are most grateful for their comments, criticisms, and insights.

Invaluable support in typing, producing, and editing this report has been given by Shirley Lithgow, Lee Meyer, and Will Harriss. A special debt is owed to Nancy Davis, who transcribed innumerable tapes, worked through untold drafts, and generally oversaw the entire effort.

Our greatest obligation is to our respondents who must remain nameless. They are found in the Office for Civil Rights, the Office of Special Education, other federal agencies, state and local educational agencies, interest groups, and concerned parties. These people gave their time and information; this report is the product of their contributions.

The flaws and misinterpretations that remain in this document can in no way be attributed to the aforementioned. Instead, the authors must blame each other.

CONTENTS

FIGURES

FIGURES

TABLES

- 1 -

I. INTRODUCTION

BACKGROUND OF THE STUDY

This is a study of the federal government's influence on local
school districts. Its immediate purpose is to identify the strategies
that the U.S. Department of Education uses to change local school
policies, and to examine how those strategies work. But its ultimate
purpose is to cast light on broader questions about the effectiveness,
costs, and benefits of federal efforts to influence state and local
governments.

Education is an appropriate focus for such an inquiry. Since 1965,
when the first major federal aid to education program was enacted,[1]
concern with creating benefits for disadvantaged groups has dominated
federal education policy. The four largest federally funded elementary
and secondary education programs have focused on (respectively) children
in low-income areas, handicapped children, children in districts
undergoing desegregation, and language minority children. These four
programs have accounted for over 90 percent of all federal aid to
elementary and secondary education.

Federal education programs typify modern American intergovernmental
relations. The federal government provides grants earmarked for
specific purposes and targeted to particular beneficiary groups.
Federal regulations establish criteria by which state and local
compliance with fiscal and service delivery requirements will be
evaluated. States and localities exercise considerable discretion in
the design and delivery of services.[2] Federal officials enforce

_____

[1] Title I of the Elementary and Secondary Education Act of 1965,
PL 89-10, 20 U.S.C. 241a et seq.
[2] The literature on intergovernmental relations is vast.
Analyses most relevant to this research include: James L. Sundquist and
David W. Davis, Making Federalism Work, The Brookings Institution,
Washington, D.C., 1969; Michael D. Reagan, The New Federalism, Oxford
University Press, 1972; and Daniel J. Elazar, American Federalism, 2d.
ed., Thomas Y. Crowell Company, New York, 1972. See also the numerous
documents issued by the Advisory Commission on Intergovernmental
Relations on the Intergovernmental Grant System: An Assessment and
Proposed Policies, Washington, D.C.

program requirements by monitoring a sample of the grantees and by investigating complaints from intended beneficiaries.

Federal grants are earmarked for specific purposes, but they create opportunities for general influence on school district policy. Congress and federal regulators can attach broad new conditions to existing grant programs. Most such conditions concern civil rights, such as nondiscrimination or preferential treatment for some disadvantaged group. School districts must either accept the conditions or do without funding for important classes of services. Congress typically assigns enforcement either to the federal agencies that administer related grant programs, or to specialized civil rights agencies. Those agencies are held responsible to detect violations, move grantees toward compliance, and punish recalcitrant local agencies by withholding funds. Such actions are inevitably controversial. Enforcement officials must walk a fine line between local agencies' complaints about federal interference and beneficiary groups' complaints about laxity or permissiveness. To avoid crippling political opposition, federal enforcement agencies must find ways to promote civil rights compliance without unduly antagonizing local officials or beneficiaries.

There is no definitive guidebook about how federal agencies should conduct themselves in trying to influence state and local units of government. Laws and regulations differ from program to program, and within programs suspected instances of noncompliance differ from one case to the next. Federal agencies are constantly developing their own institutional histories that mold the course for future enforcement activities. Compounding these factors, political crises force sudden agency reorganizations and reversals of policy. Every agency responsible for federal programs or civil rights regulations has gone through externally imposed changes in budgets, staff size, travel resources, decentralization to federal regional offices, or recentralization in Washington. Some, in addition, have had their priorities and processing deadlines dictated by court order. Federal agency strategies are, consequently, cobbled together on the run and under pressure; they do not reflect a conscious a priori design or a guiding theory. Current practice does, however, reflect a range of approaches that vary greatly in terms of obtrusiveness, effectiveness, and suitability for use in specific circumstances. A careful analysis of the existing approaches and their virtues and drawbacks should help policymakers understand what federal regulation can accomplish in education, and at what cost.

Today's political climate underlines the importance of understanding effectiveness, costs, and benefits of federal influence efforts. The Reagan Administration openly intends to reduce regulation of state and local governments. That effort, however, predates the President's electoral "mandate." Both the Carter Administration and the Democratic 96th Congress looked for ways to decrease the obtrusiveness of federal regulation and enforcement. There is no clear mandate, however, to abandon the goals that federal regulations and enforcement were intended to promote. Thus, the problem this study addresses is not partisan or transitory; everyone involved in federal regulation of social welfare programs--federal elected officials and regulators, state and local elected officials and administrators, and beneficiary group members and representatives--needs to know what it can accomplish, for whom, and at what cost.

To that end, we have studied the activities of two agencies in the U.S. Department of Education that have a great volume of enforcement-related contacts with school districts.[3] They are:

o The Office of Special Education (OSE), which manages the
   Education for All Handicapped Children program (PL 94-142).
   That program disburses $1 billion annually, primarily in
   formula grants to states as the federal government's share in
   the cost of providing individually tailored services to all
   handicapped children.

---

[3] Previous research examined the Compensatory Education Division of the U.S. Department of Education, which manages the Elementary and Secondary Education Act's Title I program. Title I is the largest federal grant program in elementary and secondary education. It provides formula grants for services to low-achieving students in low-income areas. Results of our study of ESEA Title I have been published in Paul T. Hill, Enforcement and Informal Pressure in the Management of Federal Categorical Programs in Education, The Rand Corporation, N-1232-HEW, August 1979. This report will focus on the Office of Special Education and the Office for Civil Rights, and will draw upon the results of our earlier study of Title I whenever appropriate.

o   The Office for Civil Rights (OCR), which enforces Title VI of
     the Civil Rights Act of 1964, Section 504 of the Rehabilitation
     Act of 1973, and Title IX of the Education Amendments of
     1972.[4] OCR administers no large grant programs; its mission
     is to ensure that local agencies that receive grants from such
     programs as Title I (compensatory education) and PL 94-142 do
     not discriminate on the basis of race, national origin,
     handicap, sex, or age.

We selected the two agencies because they represent a broad range
of missions, histories, funding sources, and approaches toward
influencing school districts. We observed their relationships with
school districts in order to answer the following questions:

1. How do the agencies organize and manage their staffs to develop
    objectives and priorities, identify instances of noncompliance,
    and maintain contacts with school district officials and
    beneficiary groups?
2. What tactics and incentives do the agencies use in trying to
    influence school district policies?
3. How do school districts respond to federal agencies' attempts
    to influence them?
4. What methods of influence are most and least effective, and
    most and least offensive to local officials, in what
    circumstances?

METHODOLOGY

Our basic research plan was to conduct parallel case studies of OCR
and OSE. The case study design had to produce two very different kinds
of results. First, we needed a clear picture of the two organizations'
internal workings--their missions, resources, constraints,
decisionmaking processes, and dominant values and assumptions. Second,

_____

    [4] OCR also has enforcement authority under the Age Discrimination
Act of 1975. We did not include this in our research because final
rules had not yet been promulgated at the start of this study.

we needed a good understanding of the organizations' external activities--their bureaucratic and political relationships in Washington and their interactions with the state and local agencies whose policies they are supposed to influence.

Both requirements imposed important research design problems. To create clear pictures of the two agencies' inner workings, we had to be able to resolve differences in emphases and perceptions from staff at different levels of the organizational hierarchies, and to identify latent themes and strategies that our respondents themselves might not have consciously stated. To understand OSE's and OCR's relationships with state and local agencies, we had to be able both to reconcile differences in perception and to filter out self-serving accounts of conflicts between regulators and the regulated.

We tried to solve these problems through a combination of very thorough information gathering and iterative analysis. We gathered our information, as will be explained below, through interviews at all levels of the OCR and OSE hierarchies, and in selected state and local educational agencies that have had significant, and often recent, contacts with the two federal agencies. We conducted our analysis in increments throughout the data collection process. After our first few interviews in OSE and OCR, we identified apparent themes and contradictions; we used later interviews to test and refine the themes and to search for facts that would resolve the conflicts among our sources or explain why different respondents gave contradictory reports.

We began our study with one primary assumption: Federal officials do not heavily rely on the most formal or the most punitive sanctions available for ensuring compliance--instead, they more often use informal mechanisms to influence state and local agencies.[5] Our major research task was to identify, categorize, and assess these informal influence strategies.

_____

[5] This assumption follows a growing body of literature on federal regulatory efforts. See, for example, Eugene Bardach and Robert A. Kagan, Going By the Book: The Problem of Regulatory Unreasonableness, Temple University Press, Philadelphia, 1982 (forthcoming); Hill, op. cit.; and Christopher D. Stone, Where the Law Ends, Harper and Row, New York, 1975.

Our information came primarily from face-to-face interviews conducted between September 1980 and October 1981. We met with over 150 people including high-ranking current and former political appointees and policymakers in the federal government, main-line "bureaucrats" in Washington and regional offices, national and local interest groups, state and local educational agency officials, attorneys, and complainants (see Table 1). We visited some 15 school districts, met with administrators from four state educational agencies, and conducted intensive studies of three of OCR's ten regional offices.[6] We also made dozens of telephone calls and follow-up visits to verify, clarify, or ask for further information.

Because these were elite interviews[7] we chose to make them unstructured, but we always had a list of questions to which we were seeking answers. The interviews tended to be of two types: (1) We asked the respondent to discuss his or her role in enforcing civil rights policies to get basic substantive and descriptive information, and we were particularly interested in learning about federal-state-local interactions; and (2) we posited our hypothesis that the federal government rarely undertakes formal enforcement proceedings, but gets state educational agencies (SEAs) and local educational agencies (LEAs) into compliance by using informal mechanisms--and then asked the respondents for opinions, specific instances, and experiences. We frequently found that the respondents accounts of specific instances contained implicit influence methods that they had not identified in response to our direct questions. We would then probe to see whether

---

[6] The school districts, state educational agencies, and regional offices were not randomly selected, but were chosen specifically to include regional, ethnic, financial, and size considerations. Because our data are not from randomly selected sites or respondents, we cannot claim the absolute generalizability of our results, but the patterns that emerged from our data (see discussion below) give us confidence in their widespread applicability.

[7] Lewis Anthony Dexter characterizes an elite interview as one where "the interviewee . . . is given special, non-standardized treatment. . . . [T]he investigator is willing, and often eager to let the interviewee teach him what the problem, the question, the situation is" (Elite and Specialized Interviewing, Northwestern University Press, Evanston, Illinois, 1970, p. 5).

Table 1

TYPES OF RESPONDENTS

Federal Officials (Washington)

Assistant secretaries and deputy assistant secretaries, present
  and former, of OCR and OSE
Bureau chiefs, present and former
Staff attorneys and general counsel
Departmental Congressional liaison officer
Career civil servants

Federal Officials (Regional Offices)

Regional directors
Division heads
Attorneys
Investigators
Administrators

Interest Group Representatives

Women's groups
Racial/ethnic minority groups
Handicapped groups
Education professionals, general and specialized

State Educational Agencies

Directors of special education
Monitoring staff
Federal liaison personnel

Local Educational Agencies

Superintendents and assistant superintendents
Central office administrators
Compliance specialists
Federal programs directors
Principals
Teachers

Complainants, Parents, and Beneficiary Group Representatives

they were aware of using these methods and, aware or not, how frequently they were used.

Interviews generally ran one hour in length (one lasted nearly six hours). Interest group representatives and beneficiaries eagerly responded to our requests for information. Access to officials in the federal and state governments was not a problem, although it sometimes took several telephone calls to establish contact.[8] Talking with people in LEAs was a bit more troublesome. Most were extremely hospitable and candid, but a few refused to return telephone calls or respond to letters.[9] Some of our best respondents were people who had since left their roles in the administration of federal programs and gone on to other ventures. We took notes during the interviews, which were then transcribed or summarized in memoranda. (Because our respondents were promised confidentiality, these documents are not available.) Taken together, these interviews enabled us to reconstruct histories of specific events (such as the investigation of a complaint) and to develop comprehensive knowledge of the two agencies' missions and activities.

The key element in this type of research is the identification of patterns and inconsistencies. We used patterns and inconsistencies in our respondents' description of events both to: (1) establish factually accurate accounts of particular federal contacts; and (2) draw inferences from these pieces of factual evidence to identify and categorize federal influence tactics and assess their effects on local policy. After we conducted a handful of interviews or visited one site, we reviewed and discussed our notes at length. We formulated hypotheses--for example, small school districts capitulate faster than large ones--and would test these on our next set of respondents (this particular hypothesis turned out to be unsubstantiated). Consistent patterns suggested a credible finding. Inconsistencies directed us to

_____

[8] Only one career civil servant declined to meet with us; one political appointee from the Reagan Administration also declined.

[9] We suspect their reluctance could come from several sources: uncertainty over the use that would be made of the information they were being asked to provide, suspicion of our motives, or a general lack of interest in having "outsiders" come in to do "research."

gather further information either to eliminate uncertainty or to reveal the reasons behind respondents' selected perceptions. Thus, we were constantly refining and testing our concepts and findings on each other and our respondents. There were, in the end, very few incidents for which facts and patterns of cause and effect did not emerge with clarity.

The following sections report on those clear patterns. Section II discusses the agencies' basic operating styles in terms of attitudes toward their clientele and a review of their internal processes. Section III presents a major product of this research--a typology of influence methods--and assesses the ways various strategies have been used. Section IV analyzes the local responses to federal influence efforts, and draws inferences for the broader concern of intergovernmental relations. In sum, we identified several influence methods that factor into two models of influence. We have labelled one of these "enforcement," which is the levying of sanctions; the other we have called "promotion," which involves strategic encouragement. Section V explores the effectiveness, costs, and benefits of federal efforts to influence state and local governments. It also contains a framework for choosing federal influence efforts. Despite the complexity of the research problem and the "artful" nature of the analysis, we are confident that the results are consistent and could be replicated by others. We have confidence in the "truths" produced by our research, partly because the collaborative nature of the study forced us to prove our contentions and findings to each other.

II. OPERATING STYLES AND ASSUMPTIONS

OCR and OSE are both similar and different. They are alike in
their fundamental mission--attempting to change state and local policy
on behalf of disadvantaged groups--and in the set of state and local
officials they deal with. Many of their differences are rooted in the
statutes that establish their goals and set limits on their powers and
resources. Differences established by the two agencies' founding
statutes have become accentuated over time through historical accidents
and conscious choices made by agency leadership. This section reviews
the similarities and differences in the two agencies' operating styles
under three broad headings: first, their political environments;
second, the assumptions and values that agency staff members typically
bring to their jobs; and third, internal organization and administrative
procedures.

POLITICAL ENVIRONMENT

Obviously, OCR and OSE do not operate in a political vacuum. Both
are embedded within the U.S. Department of Education, with whose goals
and purposes their own specific goals and purposes may at times
conflict. The Department of Education itself is a specialized agency
supervised by institutions with much broader political interests, i.e.,
the White House and Congress.[1] Finally, there are organized interest
groups that constantly watch, cajole, and criticize the agencies as they
pursue their missions.

On the whole, OSE's political environment is simpler and less
politically charged than OCR's. Support for education of the
handicapped cuts across all economic, ethnic, and ideological groupings.
Many members of Congress have become advocates and spokesmen for special
education; attention to the mentally and physically handicapped has been
a stated priority of several First Ladies. OSE has been able to avoid

---

[1] Classic examples of department-White House conflicts are found
in Graham Allison, Essence of Decision, Little, Brown, and Co., Boston,
1971.

unpopular decisions because Congress enacted, in PL 94-142, a fairly detailed set of requirements for education of the handicapped. The law's due process provisions also allow OSE to deflect criticism for controversial decisions away from itself and toward the courts.

OSE's relationships with interest groups are, for the most part, mutually supportive. It has placed itself in the center of provider groups and powerful organizations for the handicapped. OSE has extensive contacts with disability interest groups such as the Association for Retarded Citizens, the American Foundation for the Blind, the Association for Children with Learning Disabilities, and so forth. It is also linked to the practitioner network of special educators by grant mechanisms (see discussion below) and through professional associations, such as the Council for Exceptional Children, which has some 60,000 dues-paying members. The National Association of State Directors of Special Education (NASDSE) acts as a broker for OSE and the states by disseminating information, sponsoring workshops, and issuing policy guidance--frequently with OSE's unspoken, but financially backed, approval. NASDSE, in turn, represents the states' interests and preferences to the agency.

We found only two interest groups that have had adversarial dealings with OSE. The Education Advocates Coalition, led by the Children's Defense Fund, was formed to criticize OSE's implementation of PL 94-142, especially its compliance activities. One of the prime movers of the EAC stated: "We had to act as OSE's conscience, and we had to show them how to enforce the law." Over the years OSE has also had some antagonistic transactions with the Council of Chief State School Officers, who have questioned the need for or desirability of federal prescriptions for state special education programs.

With these few exceptions, OSE has succeeded in focusing its interactions with interest groups, Congress, and the White House on the practical problem of improving education for the handicapped. There is hardly any dispute over the goals of PL 94-142; rather, the occasional disagreement that is raised is over the specific means chosen. OSE has pursued a co-optation strategy, but its success has been founded on a genuine affinity of interest between itself and its potential critics.

OCR has a different history of relationships with other political actors. Its foundation is the vaguely worded language of the 1964 Civil Rights Act prohibiting discrimination on the basis of race or national origin. From its inception, OCR has had to make choices and decisions that have been too sensitive, unattractive, or intractable for elected officials to dictate, and has operated in a substantive area often rife with controversy and emotion. Even if the Congress, other Executive Branch agencies, and the President unanimously supported the goals of OCR's mission, the means to achieve these goals could impose enormous political costs. By virtue of its civil rights mandate, OCR is inherently more controversial than OSE. OCR's strongest allies in the Congress have traditionally been members of the Black Caucus, but it has frequently been taken to task by individual members of Congress protecting their constituencies. Other executive agencies, including the U.S. Department of Justice and several Presidents, have criticized OCR for pursuing its enforcement mission too vigorously and forgetting certain debts incurred or promises made by the administration.

OCR's relationships with interest groups representing its beneficiaries have a definite love-hate character. In addition to some of the same handicapped groups listed above, OCR has had dealings with such diverse groups as the National Organization for Women's Project on Equal Educational Rights, the Lawyers Committee for Civil Rights Under Law, the National Association for the Advancement of Colored People, and the Mexican-American Legal Defense and Education Fund. These groups have needs and grievances that go far beyond OCR's institutional powers and staff capability. Individual OCR staff and OCR's constituency groups are inevitably disappointed with the results of most of the agency's efforts. (In fact, the NAACP Legal Defense Fund filed suit against OCR, charging it with failing to implement Title VI. This suit resulted in the Adams decrees discussed below.)

Several speculations can be offered to account for these differences between OCR and OSE and other political actors. First, OSE enjoys a mission that is likely to meet very little public resistance. Because few people are so bold as to oppose the rights of handicapped children to receive public education, organizations for the handicapped start from a stronger base of support than do many of the groups attempting to influence OCR. Second, as a programmatic agency OSE has the funds to sponsor and reward effective interest groups, who therefore have an incentive for cordial and close interactions with the agency. Third, OCR may suffer by continuing to follow practices initially developed for eliminating "separate but equal" schools, although the problems of discrimination in the United States have changed over time.

STAFF ASSUMPTIONS ABOUT THEIR JOBS

Staffs of the two agencies have very different beliefs about the basic services that they are to perform. OCR sees itself as a prosecutor: Its goal is to identify violations of the law and promote justice by penalizing violators. In contrast, OSE sees itself as a facilitator of local efforts on behalf of the handicapped: Its goal is to put resources in the hands of local professionals who are trying to improve services for the handicapped. OCR is a product of the federal government's enforcement of early court-ordered desegregation that followed the Brown v. Board of Education decision in 1954. The enforcement mentality created by that experience endures, and is applied to situations that may bear little resemblance to school desegregation.

The two organizations' staffing patterns reflect their differences. OSE is staffed primarily by special education experts--persons whose original training and early job experience was in the administration and delivery of special education services. Before the enactment of PL 94-142, the special education staff in the U.S. Office of Education[2] consisted almost entirely of university-trained special education researchers. When OSE staff grew in numbers after the enactment of PL 94-142, most of the additions were drawn from the special education units of state and local governments. Even those OSE units that are dedicated to monitoring and enforcement of PL 94-142 are staffed primarily by scholars and former state special education administrators. Our interviews revealed that most OSE staff members continue to see themselves as special educators who are now practicing their profession at the federal level, rather than at the state or local levels.

---

[2] The U.S. Office of Education was in the Department of Health, Education, and Welfare.

In contrast, few OCR employees are former educators or educational administrators. Most see themselves as civil rights professionals with career lines and goals that differ dramatically from those of state and local educators. Many OCR employees are members of "affected groups"-- blacks, Hispanics, women, and handicapped persons who are attracted to OCR by the opportunity to work on behalf of the disadvantaged. Another important group of OCR employees are attorneys, many of whom were hired from other federal investigative agencies or directly from law schools after a federal court ordered a major increase in OCR's staff. These individuals also see themselves as investigative and enforcement specialists, not as educational administrators.

These different orientations are evident in the two agencies' views of their role in writing regulations to define the obligations of SEAs and LEAs. OSE's basic approach to regulation writing is expressed in the preamble to the first proposed regulations for PL 94-142, published in the Federal Register, December 30, 1976:

> Because the statute is very comprehensive and specific on many points, the Department has elected (1) to incorporate the basic wording or substance of the statute directly into the regulations, and (2) to expand on the statutory provisions only where additional interpretation seems to be necessary.

From this statement, one can conclude that OSE is averse to the "regulatory" model of influence, preferring to regulate only where it must, and then only as little as possible.[3]

OCR takes a far more aggressive approach to the drafting of regulations. It writes regulations that are considerably more precise and detailed than the authorizing statutes, uses regulation to make policy in controversial areas, and uses patterns of complaints to reveal ambiguities and loopholes in regulatory language.

---

[3] We should note that the Bureau for the Education of the Handicapped (OSE's predecessor) existed before PL 94-142 was enacted in 1975. Staff from that bureau helped to write the law, and were able to include provisions in the statute that otherwise might have been promulgated by regulations.

OCR's reliance on regulation is forced by the brevity and abstractness of the statutes it administers. The substantive guarantees in Titles VI, IX, and Section 504 are each one sentence long. Title VI is typical: "No person in the United States shall, on the ground of race, color, or national origin, be excluded from participation in, be denied the benefit of, or be subject to discrimination under any program or activity receiving Federal financial assistance." Congress clearly meant to leave the substantive definition of these guarantees to others. As things have evolved, the responsibility has been delegated to OCR.

Both OCR and OSE expect that their regulations will be used primarily as guides to voluntary local compliance actions, but neither expects that mere exhortation will be enough to guarantee the services promised to their beneficiary groups. Both expect that the regulations must be used in some cases to overcome resistance from local school board members, community leaders, administrators, or teachers.

Where the two agencies differ is in their expectations about who is to use the regulations for what purpose. OSE clearly expects the regulations to be used by local handicapped persons and their advocates. The regulations create some channels for enforcement actions in which federal officials take no part. They establish a framework of rights and procedures to be used at the local level by local people's initiative.

In contrast, OCR expects the regulations to be used by federal employees--OCR complaint investigators, Washington office staff, and administrative law judges--to determine whether particular local actions are in compliance with the law. Local beneficiaries have a role in the enforcement process as sources of complaints that stimulate OCR investigations, but the ultimate channel of enforcement is through OCR. The regulations establish a framework of rights and criteria that can be used by OCR officials either to vindicate individual rights or to send signals about federal intent.

The two agencies make very different assumptions about local officials and about the leverage enjoyed by local beneficiary groups. In general, OCR works under the assumption that local officials are not friendly to the interests of disadvantaged groups, and that local beneficiary organizations have little political leverage for protecting their interests. OSE assumes that at least some local officials (e.g., the people who administer and deliver special education services) are strongly disposed in favor of the handicapped; and that local beneficiary interest groups, especially parents of handicapped children, can promote their interests effectively. The following paragraphs explore those differences in detail.

OCR staff generally assume that local decisionmaking processes are biased against disadvantaged groups and in favor of middle-class children and their parents. These assumptions are not as unflattering as they may sound at first: OCR merely surmises that local officials are most responsive to those groups that are most numerous and pay the most taxes, and are loath to invite controversy by redirecting resources to other groups. Contrary to our expectations, OCR staff do not lump school officials together as confirmed bigots; that label is reserved for officials in the few places that have steadfastly refused to change in response to new civil rights law. OSE staff, in contrast, assume that state and local special education units are important advocates for services to handicapped children. They realize that some local officials, especially school board members, may be lukewarm about education for the handicapped because of their broader constituencies and their concern about the costs of some special education placements, but they know that most regular school employees (including principals and teachers who are glad to have special education services for handicapped children they might otherwise have to handle by themselves) are in favor of the services required by PL 94-142.

OCR staff assume that noncompliance with civil rights laws is nearly universal: School districts differ only in their degree of noncompliance. OSE staff assume that compliance with PL 94-142 is common for the most part: In all but a few school districts, the processes for proper treatment of the handicapped are in place and working.[4] This difference in perception is rooted in the two organizations' very different definitions of compliance: OCR bases its

_____

[4] However, almost every state is required to change some practices after a monitoring visit from OSE. These are largely procedural and marginal changes.

determination of compliance on behavior, while OSE focuses on processes
and plans.

OCR considers an LEA to be in compliance only if there are no
incidences of illegal discrimination. The statutes that OCR enforces
flatly prohibit discrimination in the operation of LEAs; they do not
distinguish between official local policy and particular practices that
may arise without top officials' knowledge. LEAs are required not to
discriminate, and the existence of an official policy of
nondiscrimination is not enough. Local officials must also root out
discrimination in the activities of lower-level district employees. An
LEA is not considered to be in compliance unless every employee fully
respects the rights of women, blacks, and others.

In contrast, OSE's founding statute defines compliance as a
process. A district must have a process for identifying handicapped
children, evaluating their needs and abilities, prescribing remedial
services, and delivering those services. There must also be processes
to inform parents, solicit their opinions about the child's needs, and
provide impartial review of parents' complaints. Districts are in
compliance as long as that process is present and working. Individual
children may not be getting the services they need, but the process (it
is assumed) assures that they eventually will. Districts are in
noncompliance only if that process is absent.

OCR's is a much more rigorous standard of noncompliance. It
definitely contributes to the strength of OCR staffs' contention that
noncompliance is widespread. It also makes sense of something we heard
in several interviews with mid-level OCR staff and interest group
representatives, to wit: It is safe to assume that every LEA is out of
compliance with every civil rights law. If a particular complaint about
an LEA turns out to be unfounded, a pattern of noncompliance is still
likely to prevail somewhere.[5]

_____

[5] How long these differences between the two agencies'
definitions of compliance can continue to exist is an open question.
Since 1979, OSE has been under increased pressure from several clientele
groups to look beneath processes for evidence of LEAs' actual
performance in identifying, evaluating, and serving handicapped
children. That pressure has come from many sources, including lawsuits
whose discovery processes revealed massive failures to serve handicapped
children in big-city school districts. See the discussion of court

OCR assumes that beneficiary interest groups have little leverage at the local level, and that decisions in their favor must therefore be induced by external pressure. In contrast, OSE assumes that its beneficiary interest groups have significant leverage at the local level, and that with slight improvements in organization, financing, and regulatory entitlements, those groups can obtain what they need at the local level.

Again, it is likely that both organizations are essentially right. OCR-interest group contacts are mainly at the national level, and usually between the most senior staff of the agency and the association. Among OCR's client groups, only the blacks are relatively well organized (through the NAACP and community action agencies) for political action at the state and local levels. However, the opposition to desegregation and other race-oriented issues is typically so intense that blacks are still unable to control the decisions that most directly affect them. Other groups (e.g., language minorities and women) are organized only in a few places. Language groups (other than Hispanics) and women have emphasized national, rather than local, advocacy. Most such groups also emphasize adult issues, especially employment, over elementary and secondary education. OCR has never had the funds or organizational resources necessary to help its beneficiaries organize for local political action. OCR headquarters staff therefore assume that change on behalf of its client groups must be initiated and sustained by federal pressure. OCR's assessment of beneficiaries' leverage is so low that many officials fear that individuals who complain to OCR will suffer retaliation by local officials after federal investigators leave the scene. An important rationale for keeping open the federal complaint process is the need to protect people who have appealed to OCR in the past.

OSE, on the other hand, knows that handicapped parent groups are well organized in most metropolitan areas, that statewide organizations monitor the implementation of PL 94-142, and that some were effective

cases in Philadelphia, Washington, and New York City in Michael A. Rebell, "Implementation of Court Mandates Concerning Handicapped Children: The Problems and the Potential," Journal of Law and Education, Vol. 10, No. 3, July 1981.

enough to generate passage of strong state special education laws before PL 94-142 was enacted. Every state has at least one "protection and advocacy group," funded under the federal Developmental Disabilities Act since 1973. These groups provide expert advice for local organizations, fund litigation and lobbying, and provide legal counsel for parents who wish to use PL 94-142's fair hearing procedures. Moreover, as we detail later in this section, OSE itself has done a great deal to strengthen local advocacy groups. OSE can assume that its clients are well enough organized to fend for themselves, as long as the basic PL 94-142 procedures are in place. In dealing with LEAs, therefore, OSE concentrates on maintaining the Individualized Education Programs and fair hearing processes, rather than on intervention in behalf of particular individuals.

INTERNAL ORGANIZATION AND PROCEDURES

The Office for Civil Rights

The U.S. Office for Civil Rights (OCR) was created as a result of the Civil Rights Act of 1964.[6] It is primarily an enforcement agency with jurisdiction over some 21,000 educational institutions including local school systems, state educational agencies, and colleges; to fall within OCR's scope of authority, it is only necessary that an educational agency (referred to as a "recipient") receive federal funds. OCR has the authority to ensure that no recipient discriminates on the basis of race, national origin, sex, handicap, or age.[7] The language of its authorizing legislation is almost identical for all of these substantive areas, is quite abstract, and is modeled after Title VI of the Civil Rights Act of 1964.

---

[6] An excellent history of the early days of OCR is provided in Beryl Radin, Implementation, Change, and the Federal Bureaucracy, Teachers College Press, New York, 1977.

[7] The authorities are: (1) Race and national origin: Title VI of the Civil Rights Act of 1964, 42 U.S.C. 2000-d et seq., 34 CFR Part 100, 101. (2) Sex: Title IX of the Education Amendments of 1972, 20 U.S.C. 1681, 34 CFR Part 106. (3) Handicap: Section 504 of the Rehabilitation Act of 1973, 29 U.S.C. 794, 34 CFR Part 104. (4) Age: Age Discrimination Act of 1975, 42 U.S.C. 6101 et seq.

OCR was created as a mechanism for federal Executive Branch intervention to desegregate public school systems, especially in the South. Its founding statute and subsequent regulations gave it the authority to withhold all federal funds from a recipient that is shown to discriminate. OCR's legacy--an agency born in the heyday of civil rights activism to eliminate "separate but equal" practices--persists today in its mission and operating style across all of OCR's enforcement authorities.

OCR's FY 1981 budget was nearly $47 million. There are two major levels of OCR activities. One is the administrative headquarters in Washington, D.C., currently employing some 250 staff. The central office is responsible for policy formulation, writing regulations, high-level dispute resolution, and overall management of the agency. The other level of OCR comprises the ten federal regional offices that are the primary operating arms of the agency.[8] About 750 staff are employed in OCR's regional offices to carry out the bulk of OCR's enforcement mandate in the form of complaint investigation and compliance review. These two activities are discussed below, after which we review one other responsibility of the agency.

Complaint Investigation. OCR investigates more than 2,000 complaints a year.[9] Any person or group alleging discrimination can submit a complaint to OCR. All complaints are handled initially by the regional offices; if a complaint is sent to "the government in Washington," it is forwarded to the appropriate regional office. Only two criteria must be met before OCR investigatory procedures start: (1) The basis of the complaint must be one of OCR's authorities, i.e., discrimination on the basis of race, national origin, sex, handicap, or age; and (2) OCR must have jurisdiction over the institution alleged to be discriminatory (i.e., the institution must be the recipient of federal education dollars).[10] There is also a stipulation that the

_____

[8] Organization charts and descriptions of OCR's divisions are provided in the Appendix.

[9] Federal Register, Vol. 45, No. 158, August 13, 1980, p. 53858.

[10] These criteria exclude, for example, OCR investigation of a complaint that a private school discriminates against the handicapped because there is no wheelchair ramp to its front door, when that school receives no federal funds.

alleged violation must have occurred within the past 180 days, but a waiver of this requirement is allowed at the discretion of the regional office.

Some examples from our field research illustrate the scope of OCR's jurisdiction:

o A group of parents in a middle-sized Midwestern city complained that their handicapped children were being discriminated against because they were being sent to a separate school designed for handicapped students instead of neighborhood schools.

o Two female home economics teachers in a small Southern town alleged they were discriminated against because they were paid less than male shop teachers.

o A parent of two teenaged black youths alleged his sons were not allowed to attend a particular high school and play on that school's football team for racial reasons.

o A complaint was submitted by a local interest group in a relatively wealthy Southern community claiming sex discrimination in athletic programs since there were more opportunities for boys to participate in sports than for girls.

o A "class action" complaint was submitted by a grandparent against one of the largest school systems in the United States for failing to provide education for handicapped students.

There is a very routinized system for processing complaints. The intake unit in the regional offices is the Program Review and Management Support Division which logs in complaints, checks for OCR authority and jurisdiction, and does a cursory review for completeness. If both criteria (stated above) are not met or if OCR determines that the complaint is "patently frivolous,"[11] the case file is declared

_____

[11] An example of a patently frivolous complaint from the OCR Investigative Procedures Manual is "where the complainant claims discrimination on the basis of sex, alleging that he was denied admission to a veterinary school which has a 90 percent male enrollment, while a woman who was better qualified, but had less motivation, was admitted."

administratively closed, and the process stops. Approximately 40
percent of the complaints submitted to OCR are administratively closed.
(None of the complaints listed above were closed in this fashion.)

OCR is allowed little discretion in accepting or rejecting
complaints; it is under court order to investigate all complaints that
it cannot close administratively.[12] OCR investigative activity is
further constrained by specific deadlines stated in the court order
commonly known as the Adams time lines.[13]

Assuming that OCR has authority and jurisdiction and that the
complaint is not patently frivolous, the case file is transmitted to
either the Elementary and Secondary Education Division or the
Post-Secondary Education Division of the regional office. The Division
Chief assigns the complaint to an Equal Opportunity Specialist (EOS),

_____

[12] Adams v. Califano, Civ. No. 3095-70, Consent Order, D.D.C.
December 29, 1977. The case was originally filed by the NAACP in 1970
as Adams v. Mathews, citing OCR as failing to implement Title VI. The
NAACP was joined by the Women's Equity Action League and the National
Federation for the Blind in 1981 in filing a request for a contempt of
court motion against OCR for violating the time lines. (The contempt
motion was also filed against the U.S. Labor Department's Office of
Federal Contract Compliance Programs, which also is subject to the time
lines.) Judge John H. Pratt of the U.S. District Court for the District
of Columbia found that his orders from the 1977 decision "had been
violated in many important respects" and gave OCR until August 1982 to
develop a new agreement (Cheryl M. Fields, "Court Refuses to Hold U.S.
in Contempt But Sets New Anti-Bias Deadlines," The Chronicle of Higher
Education, March 24, 1982, pp. 9-10).
    [13] The time lines are:

1. OCR must acknowledge the receipt of complaints within 15 days;
2. OCR must complete the investigation and issue findings within
    the next 90 days;
3. OCR must conduct negotiations, if necessary, within the follow-
    ing 90 days; and
4. OCR must initiate enforcement actions, if necessary, in the
    next 30 days.

The court order from Adams took the form of a consent decree between the
plaintiffs and OCR. Although the agency is significantly affected by
the consent decree, it also benefited by an increase in staff and
budget. Furthermore, it is likely that the agency is somewhat sheltered
from Presidential or Congressional attempts to limit its activities
because of the court order. Still, OCR frequently does not meet these
deadlines.

who will then have primary responsibility for the investigation and subsequent negotiations (if any). Some regional offices have their division staff divided along state lines, so a complaint from a particular state would automatically go to one of a designated group of people; other regional offices do not have this structure, and complaints are usually assigned to those whose work schedule permits.

Again, the complaint is checked for completeness and legal jurisdiction, this time by the EOS. If the complaint is not complete, the EOS contacts the complainant, usually by letter, and requests necessary information. For example, the black father who complained that his sons were prevented from transferring to a different school and thus barred from playing football on a particular team was asked if any white students in the district attended schools other than the ones they were assigned to in order to play on certain football teams.

Once these matters are in order, the EOS writes a letter (signed by the regional office director) to the school superintendent, notifying the school district that a complaint has been filed and that an investigation has been initiated.[14] The EOS then draws up an investigative plan. The plan details the data and information that will be requested from the recipient, and the ways that the data will be used to determine the validity of the complaint. Approval of the plan must be obtained from the chief civil rights attorney[15] and the regional director, after which the initial data requests are made. Some school districts that have had unpleasant previous experiences with OCR use this request to engage in game-playing. We visited one such district that had a Section 504 employment violation lodged against it. The EOS requested information on all applicants for teaching jobs over the preceding three years. In the interests of protecting the privacy of applicants, the district staff cut out all personal references from the application files that could have identified these people. OCR received boxes of forms riddled with holes.

_____

[14] This letter drew much criticism from many of our respondents in local school districts. Its tone is legalistic, citing OCR's authority, and specifics of the alleged violation are never stated. As a result, some investigations are antagonistic before they ever begin.

[15] This person heads the attorneys units found in every OCR regional office. See Appendix for details.

Once OCR has received the data, the EOS makes a preliminary analysis and determines whether a site visit is necessary. Numerous complaints are resolved during this time, while the EOS is becoming familiar with the case, because either (1) the district has decided to avoid further negotiations by taking corrective action; or (2) the EOS is convinced that an on-site investigation would not reveal patterns of discrimination (that is, that the allegation is without merit).

If the complaint is not resolved, the EOS usually attempts to conduct an on-site review. Sometimes regional directors will discourage their staff from going to the site, preferring that the matter be settled by telephone or mail. This occurs when regional directors are concerned about travel costs or unnecessary intrusion by the federal government. Most EOSs prefer to go on site visits, sincerely believing in the necessity of person-to-person communication as well as personally benefiting from the travel experience. If travel is approved, the typical site visit requires a one-day stay. During the visit more data are collected and people are interviewed, usually including the complainant, the superintendent (most often this is a brief introductory meeting), teachers or students in situations similar to those of the complainant, principals, and administrative supervisors. Sometimes interest or advocacy group members are interviewed, frequently as the result of a suggestion by the complainant.

After the on-site visit is conducted, the EOS returns to the regional office to analyze the information that was collected. The EOS makes a preliminary determination of whether a violation exists and drafts a letter of findings (LOF) for review by the regional attorneys and regional director. The letter of findings goes through the hierarchy for approval, often with several rewritings, and is sent out to the local superintendent (after clearance by the chief civil rights attorney) over the regional director's signature. (Sometimes entire case files are reviewed in depth before approval is granted.) Three types of LOFs can result from a complaint investigation:

o   No cause--there was no violation;

o   Violation corrected--the discriminatory activity has been
    voluntarily eliminated; and

o   Violation--the district is in violation, has not taken
    corrective action, and is being directed to agree to remedies
    or face penalties.

Some of the most important negotiations between OCR and the school
district take place while the LOF is being drafted and reviewed by the
OCR regional office. The EOS can make informal contact with local
officials to discuss the charges and outline OCR's possible courses of
action. Local officials who wish to avoid being found in violation of
the law can offer concessions--"voluntary" changes in their practices
that can justify OCR's issuing a "violation-corrected" letter. If these
negotiations are successful, OCR's "violation-corrected" letter will
outline remedial steps that the district has agreed to take.

A brief summary of each LOF is submitted to OCR headquarters on an
"early warning report." These reports are reviewed weekly in Washington
by representatives of OCR's central offices of Litigation, Enforcement,
and Policy; Special Concerns; and Planning and Compliance Operations
(see appendix). LOFs that determine that violations have occurred
cannot be sent out until this group and the Secretary of Education have
given approval.[16]

---

[16] Only a handful of violation LOFs have been issued under the
Reagan Administration. (We were unable to get an exact number because
OCR is now combining violation and violation-corrected letters of
findings for counting purposes.) The investigators we interviewed
thought this was consistent with the Administration's stated policy of
minimum federal intervention in local affairs, and, as a result,
investigators felt both personally and professionally pressured to
achieve resolution so that a violation-corrected LOF could be issued
(which does not need headquarters' approval). Some investigators voiced
the concern that fewer violations would be detected since the
investigative staff are held accountable for closing a specified number
of cases. A recent statement by Clarence Thomas, the Assistant
Secretary appointed by President Reagan to head OCR, summarized the new
emphasis on resolution by stating: "We can negotiate just as well
without the negative letter of findings" (Education Daily, Vol. 14, No.
212, November 4, 1981, p. 3). In short, OCR is currently following a
policy that emphasizes resolution before LOFs are issued.

If informal negotiations have failed and the OCR regional office has issued a "violation" letter, the school district has an opportunity to rebut the findings. Few districts oppose OCR at this point; instead, most begin negotiating with OCR to reach agreement on remedial actions.

In the vast majority of cases, OCR and the LEA agree on remedial action, either before or shortly after an LOF has been issued.[17] If the LEA will not agree to remedial actions, however, the case is sent to OCR's Washington Office of Litigation, Enforcement, and Policy for further action.[18] The outcomes of the investigations for the complaints listed earlier in this section are worth noting:

o   In the Midwestern case concerning placement of handicapped students in neighborhood schools, a violation-corrected LOF was issued after the state (not OCR) investigated the charge[19] and the district developed a plan to move these students into neighborhood schools.

o   The LEA that was accused of Title IX athletics discrimination received a violation-corrected LOF after the district (1) named a Title IX grievance officer; (2) agreed to put a statement on district publications that said the district did not discriminate on the basis of sex, race, or handicap; and (3) assured OCR that it would implement its school board's plan for more athletic teams for females--which had been approved before the complaint was submitted.

---

[17] Several EOSs we interviewed believe that the LOF is OCR's most potent sanction against recalcitrant school districts. More specifically, either the threat or reality of being labeled discriminatory is frequently sufficient to persuade superintendents, other district staff, or school boards of the seriousness of the matter.

[18] Theoretically, if a school district is alleged to have discriminated and refuses to cooperate with OCR's investigation, it can be immediately referred to enforcement.

[19] OCR has a stated policy that its investigations should be deferred when a complaint has also been submitted somewhere else. This policy is not always followed.

o The class action complaint against a large school system for
   failing to meet Sec. 504 standards is still in the process of
   being resolved three years after it was submitted.

o The black parent who charged that racial discrimination
   prevented his sons' transfer to another school and thus denied
   them the opportunity to play on a certain football team
   received a "no cause" letter of findings.

Once a case is sent to the litigation and enforcement office, OCR
has two options: (1) initiating administrative proceedings to suspend,
terminate, or refuse to grant financial assistance under the programs
the U.S. Department of Education administers; or (2) referring the case
to the U.S. Department of Justice for judicial action.[20] Sometimes
simply having a case referred to Washington is instrumental in getting
the LEA to agree to corrective action. Headquarters involvement
apparently intimidates some local officials; in other cases it simply
introduces new OCR officials who can break a negotiating impasse.[21]

The number of cases that go to enforcement is minuscule relative to
the number of cases handled by OCR. Only one of the complaints listed
as examples above went to enforcement (and we had to search to find
one): the charge levied by the home economics teachers that the
district violated Title IX by not paying them salaries equal to those of
shop teachers. The school district refused to change its practices

_____

[20] The U.S. Department of Justice presents the case in a district
court. Theoretically, the Assistant Secretary of OCR has the discretion
to choose between an administrative hearing or a civil suit, but in
practice this choice is made in consultation with the Secretary of
Education and the General Counsel's office. Generally, a civil suit
will be chosen instead of an administrative hearing when: (1) the
alleged violation intersects with a matter over which OCR has no
jurisdiction (e.g., housing policy); or (2) the penalty available to OCR
would be minuscule, as in some current Title IX disputes where some
courts have decided that OCR has authority only over programs receiving
Title IX funds.

[21] Some cases are pulled up from the regions because OCR has yet
to determine a policy. Recent examples include coaches' salaries
(whether men's and women's should be equal), dress codes, and "related
services" for handicapped students (what specific services--e.g.,
catheterization--are included under this broad statutory directive).

voluntarily because, as one of the district's assistant superintendents said, "We knew we were right. Shop teachers are required to work more hours than home economics teachers." The district won in court.

In most cases, both LEAs and OCR have strong incentives to resolve complaints informally. School districts prefer to avoid formal enforcement for three reasons. First, the financial and time costs involved in enforcement proceedings can severely tax the school district's resources. Second, there is a common belief among recipients that OCR will "win in court," and, in fact, that the LEA may have to take more extensive corrective actions after the enforcement proceedings than would be necessary if they settled matters with OCR out of court. One of our respondents contended that "OCR always gets its way."[22] Third, although the instances of withdrawing federal financial support are few in number, the possibility of such action is often sufficient to force the recipient to concede to OCR.

OCR, on the other hand, also has reasons for not wanting to go to enforcement. First, a case going to enforcement acknowledges that negotiation has failed, which raises doubts about the agency's skill in dealing with the school district. Second, OCR officials know that enforcement actions can attract the attention of Senators and members of Congress who might intervene on behalf of school districts in their constituencies. The memories of embarrassing situations, regardless of the time elapsed since their occurrence, are often sufficient to weaken the push to go to enforcement. One such instance was when Chicago's Mayor Daley called in a political debt from President Lyndon Johnson with regard to OCR's attempt to desegregate the Chicago school system; another was when President Ford intervened as OCR was about to forbid father-son banquets. Third, enforcement actions open OCR to scrutiny by the Department's General Counsel, who works to protect the Secretary from exposure to matters that could prove politically sensitive, embarrassing, or legally questionable. Fourth, enforcement actions can bring to the fore latent tensions between the regional offices of OCR and its Washington headquarters staff. Regional staff see themselves as

---

[22] George Eads has pointed out to us that there are parallels with the "[U.S. Department of] Justice always wins" attitude that used to be prevalent in antitrust cases.

civil rights advocates who are personally and professionally committed to eradicate discrimination in education. The regional office staff see OCR headquarters staff as administrators whose chief concern is managerial efficiency and political prudence. Regional office staff therefore try to resolve cases themselves without involving the Washington office. Lastly, the staff in OCR (especially in headquarters, but also in the regions) are cognizant of shifting political winds and the dangers of reaction against civil rights enforcement. During the early months of the Reagan Administration, they were clearly trying to maintain a low profile, according to several of our OCR respondents.

Compliance Reviews. The other aspect of OCR's enforcement mission-- compliance reviews--is remarkably similar to complaint investigations, but on a much larger scale requiring much greater efforts in terms of staff, time, and data. OCR conducts more than 200 compliance reviews annually.[23] Compliance reviews always involve on-site visits, but the procedures for data collection, analysis, and issuing findings are the same as for complaint investigations. The primary difference between complaints and compliance reviews arises from the way the investigative activity is initiated: Rather than reacting after receiving a complaint, a compliance review has OCR adopting a proactive monitoring and enforcement effort in that it is OCR who chooses the issues and sites for investigation.

Subjects and areas for compliance reviews generally are chosen in one of two ways: (1) as a result of the data collection surveys conducted by OCR; or (2) because of a number of complaints received from a given jurisdiction or on a certain topic. Of course, there are more informal routes by which compliance reviews may be initiated, such as by an interest group getting the attention of some high-level officials in the agency.[24]

---

[23] Federal Register, Vol. 45, No. 158, August 13, 1980, p. 53858.
[24] Theoretically, the threat of a compliance review could be used as a sanction against recalcitrant school districts that refused to negotiate a settlement after a complaint investigation. However, our fieldwork produced no instances where this "club" was wielded.

OCR's Office of Planning and Compliance Operations has a Surveys and Data Analysis Branch that is responsible for conducting surveys (known as the 101 and 102 surveys). In 1978 a plan was implemented for a three-year, six-survey effort. The plan calls for surveys of four kinds of districts: (1) "high interest" districts, such as New York and Chicago; (2) LEAs under court orders; (3) all applicants for funds under the Emergency School Aid Act (ESAA); and (4) randomly selected school districts. Between 5,200 and 5,500 school systems are surveyed in any given cycle, which means data are collected from some 65,000 schools. All school districts will have been sampled at least once during this planning period. The 1978 survey was four pages long and asked a range of questions on racial and ethnic composition of schools and classes, student suspensions, accommodations for physically handicapped students, pupil assignment to classes, and composition of interscholastic athletic teams.[25] The results of these surveys are published in a Directory of Elementary and Secondary School Districts, with data presented by individual schools. A list of the "100 worst" districts in any selected category is drawn up and distributed to the OCR regional offices; this list is also available to the press and the public.

Subjects of compliance reviews are chosen by the regional offices in consultation with headquarters. Many regional officials think compliance reviews make excessive demands on staff and financial resources, and would prefer not to do them. Some regional officials also fear that conducting compliance reviews would cause them to violate the complaint processing deadlines established by the Adams order.

Compliance reviews can be on a particular topic (e.g., limited English proficiency programs) or OCR can come into a school system to examine all of the issues for which it has authority. Our fieldwork showed the expansive reviews to be few in number, probably due to the pressures on EOSs to investigate and close complaints.[26]

---

[25] Interestingly, we heard claims from OCR headquarters staff that the mere appearance of a new item on the 101/102 surveys often causes corrective action at the local level. This is, presumably, because the item cues school districts as to OCR's interests.

[26] Indeed, case closures are an implicit, if not explicit, element of merit reviews for EOSs, who are expected to close some 18 to 20 complaints annually.

Pregrant Review of Emergency School Aid Act Applicants. OCR has played a part in administering the Department of Education's largest incentive grant program, the Emergency School Aid Act (ESAA).[27] That program provides approximately $300 million each year to approximately 500 school districts undergoing desegregation. The funds help support special teacher training and remedial instruction and buy equipment (e.g., buses), and are used for planning and managing the desegregation process. ESAA rewards voluntary efforts, but the bulk of its funds go to school districts that are under court orders or threatened with federal enforcement action.

ESAA funds are administered by the Office of Equal Opportunity Programs (OEOP), a Department of Education unit in Washington that is completely separate from OCR. But OCR plays a crucial role in the program. Before any district can receive an ESAA grant (or a renewal of an existing grant), OCR must conduct a general review of the LEA's compliance with Title VI. That review includes the suitability of the district's desegregation plan, but it also covers other topics such as nondiscrimination on the basis of sex and treatment of the handicapped and language minority groups. If OCR finds the district out of compliance, it can stop the award. After a finding of noncompliance, OCR participates as one of three parties (with the LEA and the OEOP) in negotiating an agreement about conditions that the LEA must meet in order to receive the grant.

The ESAA pregrant review process indirectly increases OCR's leverage in other areas. During the pregrant review, OCR combs its files to identify any recent complaints from individuals in the applicant school district. Records of the complaint investigation are attached to the district's application and reviewed by OEOP along with materials specifically prepared for the pregrant review. Among the districts we visited, one reported that an unresolved OCR complaint

---

[27] As this report is going to press, the discussion of OCR's review authority under the ESAA is largely irrelevant because this program has been consolidated into the Education Consolidation and Improvement Act's Chapter 2 (PL 97-35), which is a block grant that minimizes federal intervention. Regardless, we include a discussion of OCR's past involvement to identify and assess the agency's history of influence strategies.

figured in the ESAA pregrant review. OCR had investigated the complaint (which concerned policies for permitting white students to transfer out of desegregated schools), but had not issued an LOF. The district had, in fact, heard nothing about the complaint since the OCR field investigator obtained the tabulations he had requested and left town without commenting on the merits of the complainant's case. When OEOP raised the issue in the course of pregrant negotiations, district officials felt compelled to make concessions that the OCR investigator had not even requested.

Districts expecting an ESAA grant have an incentive to resolve any complaint investigated by OCR quickly, to keep the pregrant review free of extraneous issues. OCR, on the other hand, can rely on OEOP's pregrant bargaining leverage to resolve complaints that are too ambiguous to be closed directly in the complainant's favor. As one OCR regional official said, "ESAA reviews put the school districts into double jeopardy. If we can't prove noncompliance in a complaint investigation, we can still put pressure on them in the pregrant review."

OCR's bargaining leverage is potentially enormous. Most districts that apply for ESAA funds are badly in need of funds to pay for desegregation and thus must build their desegregation plans to meet OCR's standards. OCR's leverage is limited by a shortage of staff for ESAA pregrant reviews; most reviews, therefore, rely entirely on written reports submitted by the applicant LEA. More important, desegregation plans and federal incentive payments are sometimes negotiated at very high political levels (e.g., among Congress, the White House, and local mayors or governors), and OCR can be forced to adjust its standards to fit the case. Individual negotiations can be enormously complex.[28]

---

[28] A thorough analysis of OCR's role in ESAA pregrant review would require a far larger study than this one. The federal government's negotiations with some large Northern cities have consumed decades of time and have involved shifting casts of Congressional, Executive Branch, and local actors. The most complex such negotiation, with the city of Chicago, is now in federal court for the third time.

The Office of Special Education

The mission of the Office of Special Education and Rehabilitative Services (OSE) is to implement PL 94-142, the Education for All Handicapped Children Act, signed into law on November 29, 1975. (OSE was previously the Bureau for the Education of the Handicapped (BEH), established in the U.S. Office of Education by PL 89-750, passed in 1966. BEH became OSE with the creation of the Department of Education in May 1980.) OSE is located in Washington, employing a staff of 200. Its annual budget has just reached $1 billion, of which nearly 90 percent flows through OSE as formula grants to SEAs.

Although the federal government has long been involved in the education of handicapped students, PL 94-142 was a landmark piece of legislation consolidating the government's efforts and providing hundreds of millions of dollars for programs.[29] The law contained three salient provisions: (1) Every handicapped student is entitled to a free appropriate public education; (2) the appropriate education for each handicapped student is to be specified in a written individualized education program (IEP) drawn up by qualified special education experts in consultation with parents and renewed annually; and (3) parents (or guardians) have the right to an impartial due process hearing when they disagree with the school district's recommendation.

OSE has three primary areas of responsibility over PL 94-142. First, it administers the grant program to the states. Second, it monitors a system of state-administered procedures intended to ensure that beneficiaries get the services to which they are entitled. Third, it promotes the general improvement of special education funding, services, and practices at the state and local level. Each of these is discussed below. (See the appendix for a discussion of OSE's organizational structure.)

State Grants. By far the most visible and most important activity specified in PL 94-142 is the state grant program administered by OSE to help states meet the additional costs incurred for educating handicapped

---

[29] A good history of the enactment is found in Erwin L. Levine and Elizabeth M. Wexler, PL 94-142: An Act of Congress, Macmillan Publishing Co., New York, 1981.

students. The FY81 appropriation was $874.5 million, which is distributed to states and territories on the basis of a Congressionally specified formula. These funds cover between 8 and 12 percent of the costs incurred for educating the handicapped (a state is allowed to keep up to 25 percent of its grant for administrative expenses). Only New Mexico has declined these funds, claiming the administrative burdens of accepting this aid would be too onerous to justify participation in the program. To receive its grant a state must submit a plan detailing its implementation program. OSE must approve the state plan, which sometimes requires extensive negotiations.[30]

Monitoring. OSE's second major function is to monitor state administrative procedures required by PL 94-142. This responsibility is divided into three parts, each administered by a specialized branch of the agency's Division of Assistance to States:

o Policy development and clarification is done by the State
   Policy Branch;

o Receipt and processing of data on the number of beneficiaries,
   approval of the state plan, subsequent award of funds, and
   technical assistance are the responsibility of the Field
   Services Branch. Its primary concern is that federally
   prescribed elements of the program have been established (most
   of which are procedural, such as signed assurances and public
   notification activities); and

o On-site monitoring of SEAs is performed by the Compliance and
   Enforcement Branch.

Of OSE's activities and responsibilities, its on-site monitoring comes closest to the OCR enforcement model. Perhaps more than any other function in the agency, on-site monitoring has gone through changes in emphases and ways of doing business. Its evolution over the past few years has been toward more rigorous monitoring. Current plans call for monitoring to begin with a much greater use of data and information (some will be provided by OCR) prior to the visit, to develop a "state

---

[30] OCR must also give its approval of the state plan, which is a new procedure. See the section on "Interagency Coordination," below.

profile" for each SEA. The monitoring visits will focus on how a state performs its own monitoring function, which is not too different from the focus of past efforts, but an additional investigative effort will come from using the state profile to target specific problem areas for on-site scrutiny (e.g., least restrictive environment and child-find efforts).

It is unclear, however, whether the trend toward more rigorous monitoring will continue. OSE recently received harsh criticism from members of Congress and the Reagan Administration over the results of a conflict with the California SEA. OSE is therefore balancing between its vocal beneficiaries and their interest groups, and a set of watchful politicians and political appointees. OSE's new sensitivity over criticism of its aggressive monitoring was symbolized by changing the name of the state response to an OSE monitoring visit from a "voluntary compliance plan" to a "voluntary implementation plan."

Promoting Improvement of Special Education. In addition to the state grant program, OSE administers the following discretionary grant programs intended to improve local special education practice:

Program	FY81 Funding (in $ thousand)
State assistance	
Preschool administrative grants	$25,000
Deaf-Blind Centers	16,000
Special population programs	
Severely handicapped projects	4,375
Early childhood education	17,500
Regional, vocational, adult, and postsecondary programs	2,900
Innovation and development	15,000
Media and resource services	
Media and captioned films	17,000
Regional resource centers	7,656
Recruitment and information	750
Special education personnel development	43,500
Special studies	1,000

Funds from these programs--totaling over $150 million annually-- are distributed to SEAs, LEAs, colleges, and beneficiary organizations. OSE distributes the funds on a discretionary basis, relying on peer review panels (rather than fixed formulas) to identify grantees. To show the breadth of OSE's grant activities, some examples of the specific use of these funds are discussed below.

OSE makes annual grants to the National Association of State Directors of Special Education (NASDSE), which supplies a critical linkage between OSE and state governments. NASDSE is the medium through which OSE creates and issues informal policy guidance to the states. OSE routinely informs NASDSE about negotiations with states; NASDSE then disseminates results of OSE state monitoring visits to all state directors. NASDSE has three grants from OSE totaling about $300,000 annually.

OSE's Division of Personnel Preparation awards grants to improve the quality and increase the supply of special education personnel. Primary beneficiaries of its grants are higher educational institutions. This Division's FY81 budget was $43.5 million, although there was a rescission of $15 million effective June 1981. FY81 funds were distributed among higher education institutions (73 percent), SEAs (10 percent), LEAs (4 percent), and other nonprofit organizations (13 percent). Among the nonprofit organizations are 17 local parent advocacy training groups that promote the active use of PL 94-142's IEP and due process provisions.[31]

Other major OSE grants are to "Closer Look," a national resource center for parents, handicapped adults, practitioners, students preparing for teaching in special education, and advocates; 12 Regional Resource Centers that assist schools and local educational agencies by evaluating the educational quality of programs for handicapped students

_____

[31] Interestingly, the Congress specifically protected the parent groups in the recent budget rescission, stating that their funding was not to be cut.

($7.5 million per year); and 12 Direction Service Centers that help LEAs and parents to match handicapped students' needs with available services ($2 million annually).

INTERAGENCY COORDINATION

It is possible that the operating styles and assumptions of OCR and OSE may be converging. There is an obvious area of overlap between the two agencies for ensuring nondiscrimination for handicapped students.[32] Coordination was largely informal until the Department of Education was being formed, at which time the Secretary created a task force "to review criticisms and recommend policies and procedures" concerning equal educational opportunities for the handicapped. The task force had members from the Education Department's Deputy Under Secretary, OSE, OCR, the Office of the General Counsel, Compensatory Education, and the Department of Justice.

The primary source of criticism was a document issued on April 16, 1980,[33] produced by the Education Advocates Coalition, a group spearheaded by the Children's Defense Fund.[34] The report charged a systematic failure on the part of states and localities to deliver services required under PL 94-142. It demanded more aggressive monitoring from OSE for state and local compliance, and that OSE coordinate its proposed reviews and complaint investigations with OCR's enforcement of Section 504 guarantees.[35]

---

[32] About one-half of the complaints currently received by OCR are on the basis of Sec. 504.

[33] In a deliberate effort to influence federal policy, it was no coincidence that the report was issued the day before Edwin Martin was named Assistant Secretary to head OSE. Martin had previously been the Commissioner of the Bureau for the Education of the Handicapped (OSE's predecessor).

[34] Report by the Education Advocates Coalition on Federal Compliance Activities to Implement the Education for All Handicapped Children Act (PL 94-142), April 16, 1980.

[35] A careful reading of the Education Advocates Coalition (EAC) report suggests that many of the activities demanded of OSE were not

A memorandum of understanding was signed on October 15, 1980, that, among other things, called for:

o   Joint OSE/OCR pregrant compliance reviews and joint evaluations of state PL 94-142 plans;

o   Referral of all citizen complaints to OCR for investigation under Section 504, if applicable;

o   Sharing data between the two offices, especially from the OCR 101/102 forms; and

o   Increased use of performance data--e.g., numbers and proportions of children served under PL 94-142, size of waiting lists for special education placements, and disproportionate placements of minority students in classes for the mentally retarded--as triggers for compliance reviews.

It is too early to assess the impact of the memorandum. "Point men" have been designated in both agencies, who coordinate all contacts and interactions. The agencies have conducted one joint review (in Ohio), but an LOF has not been issued as of this writing. OCR has reviewed some PL 94-142 state plans, and has caused some state funds to be delayed, usually because due process procedures have been inadequate.

The memorandum of understanding and the pressures that produced it have reduced the differences between OCR's and OSE's definitions of compliance. OSE has now built a small staff of enforcement specialists, and its more aggressive investigations of state and local compliance have led it to suspend grants to several states and to negotiate important changes in several states' special education plans. At this time, OSE still has not abandoned its original focus on the maintenance of processes rather than the guarantee of specific services to individual beneficiaries. However, several top-level OSE staff

_____

consistent with its authorizing statutes, but were consistent with OCR's. Yet, it was OSE that was the object of dissatisfaction, with the EAC urging that agency to adopt a compliance model much more like that of OCR. The reader is left with the impression that the substantive concerns voiced in the report may have been secondary to its symbolic value--chastising an agency and a new assistant secretary that had previously received broad acclaim.

expressed skepticism about whether the PL 94-142 planning and complaint processes have been sufficient. These staff attitudes, reinforced by proddings from handicapped advocacy groups and scrutiny by OCR, will continue to be sources of pressure on OSE to conduct strict scrutiny of state and local performance.

This section has reviewed the similarities and differences in OSE's and OCR's operating styles in terms of their political environments, staff assumptions and values, and internal administrative procedures. The next section identifies the techniques used by the two agencies to influence state and local educational agencies.

III. INFLUENCE METHODS

This section reports our findings on OCR's and OSE's efforts to influence local educational policy. Like Sec. II, it relies on comparisons between OCR and OSE. The comparisons, however, are not presented only for descriptive purposes: Our goal is to understand the influence strategies inherent in OCR's and OSE's actions toward school districts. To do that, we must look beneath the two agencies' actions to identify the incentives and pressures that those actions are supposed to create. This section has three parts. The first establishes a typology of influence methods that we have discovered by observing OSE and OCR. The second part explains how the different influence methods are supposed to work, and provides concrete examples of how OCR and OSE use them. The third part summarizes the differences between the two agencies and identifies the different models of federal influence that are implicit in their activities.

A TYPOLOGY OF INFLUENCE METHODS

As Sec. II has shown, the two agencies' missions and organizational processes differ in many ways. Close examination revealed, however, that their methods for influencing educational agencies overlap a great deal. Despite statutory and historical differences, the agencies appear to have access to remarkably similar means of applying pressure on school districts. (For example, both agencies have used the threat of funding cut-offs to effect compliance, and both have encouraged beneficiaries to use local publicity to prod local officials to change certain practices.) The two agencies differ only in the specific use of the influence methods and in the relative emphasis they place on them.

Table 2 lists the agencies' main influence methods--and the order in which they are presented reflects a major finding of the study. We conclude that the influence methods themselves are components of two broader strategies of influence. The first such strategy is enforcement, which relies on federally administered sanctions to create changes in local policy. The second strategy is promotion, which relies on local supporters of federal program goals to act on their own behalf, with the federal government providing resources (funds, organization, and guidance) to enhance the effectiveness of local supporters' actions. In Table 2, the first three influence methods are components of the enforcement strategy and the last five of the promotion strategy.

The next subsection explains how OSE and OCR use each method and how each is meant to influence state and local educational policy. The final subsection will show how the specific methods fit into the larger strategies of enforcement and promotion. Our intention here is to describe and compare OCR's and OSE's actions in order to reach a more general understanding of the influence methods available to the federal government; we defer discussion of the agencies' overall effectiveness to Sec. IV.

OSE AND OCR INFLUENCE METHODS
Threat of Corporate Penalties

Corporate penalties--the reduction of state or local agencies' income through fines or withholding of future grant funds--are the bedrock of the enforcement process. Without the prospect of corporate penalties, federal agencies would be powerless in the face of defiance of their regulations, and federal site reviews and complaint investigations would have little meaning. Other influence methods to be discussed later (e.g., process costs and individual sanctions) ultimately depend on the threat of corporate penalties.

The two agencies have very different procedures for imposing corporate penalties. If OSE concludes that a state educational agency (SEA) is out of compliance, it can petition the Secretary of Education to suspend the state's PL 94-142 grant. OSE proposes an amount to be withheld and suggests whether the suspension will affect the entire PL 94-142 grant or only the 25 percent earmarked for state discretionary expenditures.

OCR must present the results of complaint investigations in a U.S. District Court or before an impartial administrative law judge in an open adversary hearing. If an administrative law judge confirms OCR's finding of noncompliance, OCR recommends a penalty, which the Secretary may or may not impose. Federal courts impose their own penalties. OCR

Table 2

INFLUENCE METHODS AVAILABLE TO OCR AND OSE

Threat of corporate penalties: threatened decreases in the local agency's income through imposition of fines or withholding of future grants.

Individual sanctions: increases in personal stress or potential damage to the careers or incomes of local officials who must respond to federal enforcement or local complaints by beneficiaries.

Process costs: imposition of demands for expenditure of time and money to keep records, make reports, cooperate with federal monitoring, rebut charges, appeal the imposition of penalties, or respond to demands by beneficiaries.

Corporate rewards: increases in local agencies' income through discretionary grants or prizes.[a]

Individual rewards: increases in incomes, satisfaction, reputations, or career prospects of local officials who promote local compliance with federal requirements.

Technical assistance: help in implementing policy changes required by regulation by providing expert advice, staff training, self-assessment manuals, and models of compliant local programs.

Encouraging beneficiary organizations: helping beneficiary groups to organize at the national, state, and local levels by providing subsidies to such groups or requiring state and local governments to establish them.

Creating leverage for beneficiaries and advocates: establishment of specific beneficiary rights to obtain information about, be consulted about, approve, or contest local policy decisions.

---

[a]The typology excludes formula grants because they can be created only by Congressional statutes and appropriations, and are therefore not given at the discretion of federal agencies.

typically recommends a penalty that corresponds to the amount of federal funds spent by the local educational agency (LEA) while it was out of compliance. (Theoretically, OCR could propose that all federal education funds received by the LEA be withdrawn.) The Secretary, however, typically imposes a far lower penalty, or none at all, after discussions with the LEA, its SEA, and Congressmen from the affected areas. OCR can also create corporate penalties through the Emergency School Aid Act's pregrant review process, as explained in Sec. II.

Despite their fundamental importance, corporate penalties are rarely imposed. OSE, for its part, has never penalized a state by reducing its PL 94-142 grant. It has, however, conducted complex-- and reportedly very stressful--negotiations with several states, and produced significant changes in those states' special education policies, sometimes by delaying the PL 94-142 grants until appropriate adaptations were promised or obtained. Though states' PL 94-142 allocations are determined by statutory formula, and delays do not ultimately reduce the affected state's income, the disruptions in cash flow entail important costs. If PL 94-142 funds are delayed, the SEA must either arrange large cash advances from other state accounts or temporarily reduce grants to LEAs. Local school districts whose grants have been delayed must either lay off special education staff or temporarily pay for special education services out of other accounts. The administrative arrangements at all levels are extremely complex, and must be explained at length to affected administrators, teaching staff, and parents.

OCR's use of corporate penalties is also rare. In the past five years, only 13 cases have been sent to the Department of Justice for prosecution in district court, and 60 cases have been brought before an administrative law judge by OCR.[1] The last time OCR imposed a

----

[1] It would be interesting to know what percentage of complaints these figures represent. However, OCR's records are incomplete, so we must estimate this percentage. In FY81, OCR investigated about 1,500 complaints, so we believe it would be conservative to estimate that OCR conducted 5,000 complaint investigations and compliance reviews over the past five years. If this estimate is accepted, it means that less than 1 percent of all investigated complaints or compliance reviews move to judicial proceedings.

financial penalty was in 1972 against the Ferndale, Michigan, school
system.[2]

Corporate penalties are rare for several reasons. First, they can
be imposed only after the complex and laborious processes outlined
above. Second, proposed penalties often generate powerful political
counterpressures; as a result, final decisions about penalties are often
affected by issues which, from the point of view of OSE and OCR, are
unrelated to the case at hand. Classic examples of these "unrelated
issues" are when the Congress or the White House pressures Executive
Branch agencies to go easy on school districts. Third, fiscal penalties
often threaten to harm the very local beneficiaries on whose behalf they
are imposed: If a state or locality has to pay a fine or suffer
reductions in federal grants, services to disadvantaged groups are
likely to be cut.[3] Finally, corporate penalties are the harshest
sanction available to federal agencies, and their very use signifies the
failure of negotiations.

Though corporate sanctions are seldom imposed, they are a factor in
most transactions between federal agency employees and local officials.
Contrary to other evidence, many local officials appear to assume that
corporate sanctions are readily available to their federal counterparts,
and likely to be applied if negotiations fail. Our interviews revealed
that local officials had minimal knowledge of the arduous steps OCR and
OSE must follow to impose a penalty; they focused instead on the value
of the largest fine that the federal agency could recommend. The
prospect, however remote, of major disruptions in local services caused
by a corporate penalty was often too fearsome to be risked.

_____

[2] As this report is going to press, OCR has announced it will cut
off all federal funds received by the Perry County, Mississippi, school
district. OCR has charged the district with racial discrimination and
retaliation against the complainants; the district maintains it has not
acted improperly, bolstered by a ruling in its favor from the state's
supreme court (Charles R. Babcock, "U.S. Halts Aid to Mississippi School
District," The Washington Post, March 19, 1982, pp. A-1, A-10).
[3] For a full discussion of the problems of imposing corporate
penalties, see Hill, Enforcement and Informal Pressure in the Management
of Federal Categorical Programs in Education, The Rand Corporation,
N-1232-HEW, August 1979.

Penalties against SEAs and LEAs being rare enough to be highly newsworthy, local officials vividly remember the few stories about them that they have heard or read about. The complexity of the sanctions process may also work in the federal government's favor. Fiscal sanctions get their greatest publicity when they are proposed; though most penalties are drastically reduced if not dropped altogether in the final negotiations between the Secretary's office and the SEA or LEA, the sanction everyone remembers is the one first proposed by the investigating agency.

Some federal investigators deliberately exaggerate the probability of such penalties. One OCR complaint investigator threatened to cut off an LEA's ESAA grant "just by picking up the telephone." Others claimed to be unable to prevent the imposition of penalties once higher-ups (e.g., the OCR regional office director or Washington headquarters staff) entered the picture. Such threats have also been effective for OSE staff in their negotiations with SEAs, especially after the recent brief suspension of California's PL 94-142 grants. These tactics appeared to work even when negotiators representing the SEAs and LEAs should have been relatively sophisticated. One LEA lawyer reported that he decided to make concessions after an OCR investigator threatened an immediate cut-off of federal funds. By calling attention to past instances of corporate sanctions and by bluffing to increase local officials' perception of risk, federal negotiators ensure that the slight prospect of corporate sanctions casts a long shadow.

There is, of course, a need to maintain the perception of threat by imposing some real penalties. Because OSE's actions against California are so recent, state officials we interviewed definitely believed sanctions were possible. At the time of our fieldwork, the credibility of OCR's sanctions was eroding because of serious questions about whether the Reagan Administration would allow any penalties for civil rights violations.[4] In one of the LEAs we visited, a district's

---

[4] As mentioned above, OCR has just announced that it is imposing a corporate penalty against Perry County, Mississippi. Obviously, it is difficult to anticipate how this penalty could affect other school districts.

assistant superintendent has told OCR that "our response to civil rights issues is affected by the weakness of the feds' enforcement posture." Most districts, however, still assume that fiscal sanctions can result from any transaction with OCR.

From our analysis, it is clear that OSE and OCR are forced to seek corporate penalties when an instance of noncompliance is so serious and flagrant that failure to punish it would encourage noncompliance elsewhere. The agencies seek penalties whenever the failure to do so would threaten their own credibility, but they are subject to political pressures from higher-level actors that can restrict their efforts. One OCR regional office we visited had put only two LEAs through formal administrative hearings in the past two years; in both cases the alleged offense was retaliation against individuals who had submitted complaints to OCR. The agencies must display their willingness to "go to the mat"--even if only occasionally and under extreme pressure--in order to maintain the background level of threat that makes other influence methods possible.

Corporate Rewards

Corporate rewards (usually in the form of incentive grants) can provide extra income to school districts that make exemplary efforts to comply with federal requirements. Local decisionmakers presumably try to win the reward by providing especially good services for federal program beneficiaries. The extra income provided by incentive grants can be used to support compliance-related activities or for more general purposes. Restrictions on the use of such funds affect their effectiveness as incentives: Grants with no use restrictions are highly attractive to school board members and superintendents, while restricted grants are more attractive to officials who are responsible for administering specific compliance activities.

OCR administers no real corporate rewards for school districts. The limited amount of funds that OCR has available for discretionary grants are usually spent on support for beneficiary interest groups or for university-sponsored demonstrations or development activities. (OCR's role in the administration of ESAA grants was previously discussed under corporate penalties.)

OSE, unlike OCR, has direct administrative responsibility for a number of incentive grant programs. Yet OSE rarely uses the implicit opportunity to negotiate specific changes in local policy. For example, OSE administers a $21 million program of annual grants for deaf and blind centers. These funds are intended to help SEAs and LEAs to upgrade their services for deaf and blind children. Grants are awarded competitively, based on purely technical criteria, and proposals are evaluated by professional review panels, not by OSE staff. Applicants are not subject to any special pregrant compliance review. OSE negotiates with SEAs and LEAs only to obtain technical changes recommended by the review panel.

OSE's abstention from using potential bargaining leverage reflects its basic approach to changing state and local priorities. OSE focuses monitoring efforts at the state level and indirect influence at the local level. OSE provides educational institutions with money and technical resources, and relies on beneficiary groups and local insiders (e.g., special education staff) to create specific pressures for compliance. To imitate OCR's use of the ESAA pregrant review process would require direct negotiations between OSE staff and state and local officials. That would create tensions OSE would rather avoid.[5]

Process Costs

SEA and LEA officials know that federal investigations make demands on their staffs, that fighting to avoid or reduce penalties costs both time and money, and that it therefore pays to cooperate with OSE and OCR. That knowledge, then, endows both OSE and OCR with leverage. The process costs they can impose, however, are very different. OCR can usually impose far greater ones and can impose a variety of process costs, either directly through its demand for information or

---

[5] As discussed earlier, OSE's primary responsibility is administering a grant program to the states. We have specifically ruled out formula grants as a type of corporate reward since they are created by statute, not agency discretion. However, the concessions that a state may have to make to obtain its PL 94-142 grant may create an impression of a "corporate reward" for a job well done. At a minimum, the grants made under this program are more like corporate rewards than certain block grants (e.g., revenue sharing).

negotiations, or indirectly through its effects on school districts' decisionmaking. Though few school districts have contacts with OCR as often as once a year, OCR is a considerable presence for the larger districts in metropolitan areas. One district in our sample reported OCR investigations of more than 40 complaints in the past two years; and for some districts, one transaction with OCR can dominate the local agenda for months at a time.

OCR's compliance reviews and complaint investigations can impose the following kinds of process costs:

Collection and Reporting of Special Data. OCR initiates most of its complaint investigations and compliance reviews by requesting special data on district activities. In one district we visited, a complaint from the parents of a handicapped child about transportation arrangements led to an OCR request for the daily transportation schedules for every child in the school district. In another district, OCR officials preparing for a compliance review on suspensions of minority students asked for records of every disciplinary action taken against any secondary school student in the past year. Such data are almost never kept routinely, and must therefore be specially collected and reported. Though districts are often able to persuade OCR to pare down its data requests (the two districts cited above were able to provide sample data on a more focused set of questions than OCR posed initially), local staff members still must spend many days assembling data.

Cooperation with OCR's Fact-Finding Visits. Compliance reviews normally require site visits of 1 to 5 days duration. Though some complaints can be investigated by inspection of written records, many require site visits of 1 to 2 days. During site visits, senior local staff typically must rearrange their schedules to accompany the OCR site visitors, answer questions, and arrange meetings with school personnel.

Negotiation. Should OCR's investigators find in favor of the complain"vant, the LEA faces the possibility of several rounds of negotiations. First, the OCR investigator suggests a compliance agreement that will eliminate the need for any enforcement action. Second, the investigator's regional office director can initiate official negotiation, again offering to stop enforcement action in return for specific "voluntary" actions by the school district. Finally, in the unusual instance where negotiations are unsuccessful, OCR Washington office staff (often high-ranking officials such as the Assistant Secretary or Deputies) can initiate further discussions. These can involve local Congressional representatives, mayors, and governors.

Every stage of this negotiation process may impose great costs in time, emotion, and energy, and local officials can expect to spend many hours on the telephone and drafting letters. Costs become especially high when high-ranking federal officials become involved; then the superintendent's schedule, as well as the schedules of deputy superintendents and the local school district's attorneys, are preempted by the negotiations.

Conducting Internal Consultations. Most districts, when found out of compliance by an OCR investigator, offer to make some policy changes in return for a "violation-corrected" finding. This imposes additional costs of internal consultations. Local school district negotiations can only make agreements in areas covered by their own authority, and they must get higher-level support for agreements that require new funds or changes in service patterns. In some cases, internal consultations become very complex because they spill over the normal lines of administrative accountability. It can, in fact, become necessary for school officials to touch base with and reassure almost every active constituency. As one school official told us, "When OCR pushes for change in one area, then all the parent groups become nervous and vigilant. They are afraid that we will promise something that costs money, and that we will take the money away from their school or their kids. An OCR investigation arouses everybody, even if it is focused on a relatively narrow issue."

Participating in Administrative Hearings and Litigation. Though only a tiny fraction of cases ever get to formal administrative hearings or litigation, those that do are likely to be protracted for years. Such processes seldom lead to the imposition of large fines, and school districts facing large penalties are often willing to trade process costs for potential fiscal penalties. But for LEAs facing small penalties or modest costs of coming into compliance, it is often far cheaper to accede to OCR's demands than to endure the process costs.

Because they dread paying process costs, many school districts make
changes in policy as soon as they become aware of a complaint or of
OCR's plan to investigate a particular issue in a compliance review.
One regional OCR official estimated that one-fourth of all complaints
are settled before OCR's formal investigation begins by officials hoping
to avoid the "hassle" of dealing with OCR.

Process costs are implicit in every contact between a federal
compliance officer and a state or local administrator. The contact
itself is a process cost, and any feature of the interaction that might
create the need for additional contacts is a potential source of more
process costs. Such costs are, however, reciprocal. Federal officials
have limited time and energies, and agendas that can be disrupted.
State and local administrators can therefore impose process costs of
their own.

A good illustration of the reciprocity of process costs can be
taken from the typical interaction between an OCR complaint investigator
and the local officials whose activities he is investigating. By his
very presence, the federal official threatens to impose the process
costs identified above--data collection, negotiation, internal
consultation, administrative hearings, and litigation. However, the
federal investigator also has a caseload of complaints to be
investigated, and if a particular case requires repeated telephone
calls, letters, and negotiations with his OCR superiors, the
investigator falls behind schedule. Further, as we learned from OCR
regional office staff, local officials can impose process costs by
introducing complications that require investigators to seek clearance
or approval from higher levels in OCR.

OCR investigators cannot formally charge LEAs with noncompliance or
initiate enforcement actions without extensive review by their
superiors. Any LOF that identifies a major uncorrected violation
requires extensive documentation, several levels of review of the case
file, and an oral quizzing of the investigator by the regional legal
staff. The investigator must prepare the case files for review in
Washington. If anyone--the Washington office, the regional director, or
the chief regional civil rights attorney--thinks the file is incomplete,

the investigator must request more facts and revise the findings and analysis. If the Washington office decides to negotiate directly with the school district, the investigator must prepare the file for others' use and be available to answer their questions. These procedures reduce the investigator's control over his or her own time. They also expose his or her work to unwelcome criticism and second-guessing.

The ability to impose process costs on one another creates a commonality of interest between OCR investigators and local officials. Both strongly prefer to close any investigation by reaching an agreement between themselves. That is easy, of course, if the investigator finds no evidence of noncompliance. If the investigator finds a violation, both sides have a strong incentive to agree on a remedy so the case can be closed with a "violation-corrected" letter. If the parties find themselves in real disagreement, they must weigh the importance of their disagreement against the likely process costs of pursuing it further.[6]

Senior OCR officials worry that investigators will overlook problems rather than report noncompliance and initiate further enforcement actions. They try to eliminate false findings of compliance by training staff, spotchecking investigators' reports, and remaining open to complaints from beneficiary groups. But they must ultimately rely on the investigators' own commitment to civil rights issues.

OSE imposes almost no process costs directly on LEAs. OSE monitors may visit three or four local districts per state every third year. Otherwise, they request no data and conduct no negotiations. Indirectly, however, OSE's program can impose considerable process costs through procedural requirements, due process hearings, or lawsuits under PL 94-142.[7]

---

[6] Such a bargaining relationship between investigator and respondent is common to any form of law enforcement. Police officers, for example, face significant process costs when they arrest an individual rather than ignore an offense or create rough justice on the spot.

[7] Though these costs are not well documented, available estimates are that a single due process hearing can require an average of 62 person-hours' preparation by LEA employees, and cost an average of about $3,000 for hearing officers' fees, legal representation, transcripts, etc. (Some data on the process costs imposed by PL 94-142 hearings are provided by Roland K. Yoshida, "Developing Assistance Linkages for Parents of Handicapped Children," U.S. Department of Education, Bureau for the Education of the Handicapped, Washington, D.C., 1980 (mimeo);

Most of OSE's direct contacts are with SEAs; and though OSE
traditionally prefers collegial negotiations over any forms of pressure,
it can impose process costs that make life difficult for state
officials. Most such costs are imposed in the context of the renewal of
the state's special education plan, done once every three years. If OSE
is unhappy with the state plan or believes, based on its site visits,
that the SEA is unlikely to live up to all of the assurances given in
the plan, it can request voluminous additional data and analyses.
Special education administrators in one SEA reported that it took nearly
a year to get OSE approval for its previous three-year plan. As one
official put it, "They demanded so many reports and called so often on
the telephone to ask for clarifications that we finally said, 'Just tell
us what you want and we'll do it.'"

An additional process cost that OSE imposes on SEAs is the agency's
separate monitoring and enforcement functions. As discussed in Sec. II,
these visits take place at least once every three years, when a team
from Washington comes in to review countless aspects of special
education policies and practices. If OSE is not satisfied, it can
delay, and has delayed, a state's formula grant funds. States can do
little to eliminate the process costs from either the plan review or
monitoring efforts of OSE because these are routine, recurring federal

---

and Howard B. Casmey, "Report to the 1981 Session, Minnesota State
Legislature, on Impact of the 1979 Amendment to Minn. Stat. 102117 subd.
3b, Education of Handicapped Children," Minnesota Department of
Education, St. Paul, 1981. Their estimates, however, are loose and
reflect the experience of only a few jurisdictions.) These costs can be
much higher for cases that are appealed to the state or end up in court.
Relatively few districts actually pay these costs: The average district
handles less than one due process hearing per year. That fact is
misleading for two reasons, however: First, many districts accede to
parents' demands rather than pay the price of a due process hearing. A
service request that costs less than $3,000 is cheaper to accede to than
to fight, especially if there is any chance that the parent would win
anyway. Second, the vast majority of hearings are concentrated in a few
places. (For example, half the PL 94-142 due process hearings ever
conducted in California took place in only one of the state's 1,044
school districts; see Michael W. Kirst and Kay A. Bertken, "Due Process
in Special Education: An Exploration of Who Benefits," unpublished
research, Stanford University, n.d.) Thus, for some districts, the
aggregate process costs of PL 94-142 hearings may be very high.

interventions,[8] but they can minimize the costs by acceding to OSE preferences.

Technical Assistance

The laws administered by OCR and OSE establish broad principles (i.e., "appropriate" services for the handicapped and "nondiscrimination" for minority groups, women, and the handicapped) without providing precise operational definitions. Even the most detailed regulations cannot apply those general principles to every local case. Some local failures to comply with federal education requirements may be due as much to uncertainty about what is to be done as to any intention to deny beneficiaries their rights. Compliance is partly a learning process whereby local officials and beneficiaries discover what federal requirements mean. Federal agencies can influence local agencies by expediting and directing the learning process.[9] Both OSE and OCR provide technical assistance, but it is a very important part of OSE's activities, and only a minor part of OCR's. The agencies' budgets show this difference: OSE has $200 million to award in discretionary grants, whereas OCR has $5 million. Technical assistance is, in fact, the chief activity of OSE's Washington office staff. More than half of OSE's professional staff members work on research, development, demonstration, and dissemination; in contrast, only a handful of OSE's staff members work in the branches that write regulations, evaluate state special education plans, and review compliance.

OSE's approach to technical assistance is highly sophisticated. Consistent with its generally nondirective philosophy, OSE avoids creating any impression that its technical assistance is meant to influence local policy in any particular way. It often arranges for independent organizations (e.g., universities) to design and manage

---

[8] This is different from the local school district-OCR relationship since school districts could, at least theoretically, avoid OCR process costs by behaving in nondiscriminatory fashion.
[9] See Richard F. Elmore and Milbrey W. McLaughlin, "Strategic Choice in Federal Education Policy: The Compliance-Assistance Trade-Off," in Milbrey W. McLaughlin and Ann Lieberman (eds.), National Society for the Study of Education Yearbook, University of Chicago Press, forthcoming.

technical assistance; OSE also insulates its own technical assistance specialists from its enforcement units. OSE's field services staff review preliminary drafts of state special education plans and send comments directly to state officials; they only informally advise the other staff who conduct compliance reviews. The field services staff readily respond to requests from SEAs for assistance. We came across one recent instance where an OSE staff member provided a state trying to implement a small portion of its plan with eight successful examples already in use by other states.

Though OSE pays for the preparation of technical assistance documents (manuals, course descriptions, case histories of successful projects, etc.), they are written by independent grantees and disseminated without OSE's endorsement or criticism.[10] Consultants and workshops are arranged by LEAs and SEAs; OSE provides grant funds for those purposes but allows others to select their own topics and providers. In general, OSE treats technical assistance as a locally controlled professional activity, which is only facilitated by federal funds. This avoids the pitfalls encountered by other federal technical assistance programs, which local officials often decide are irrelevant to their needs or resent as unsubtle federal manipulation.

We have no direct evidence about how these activities affect such key state and local policies as special education appropriations, service quality, or compliance with PL 94-142 requirements. It is clear, however, that OSE-funded technical assistance activities give special education staff and teachers many opportunities for professional communication and renewal. Such activities may help maintain local special education staffs as cohesive forces in local school politics, and probably improve the performance of individual professionals.

In contrast, OCR's technical assistance activities are very limited. Lacking funds for major external grants programs, OCR can provide few of the training sessions, manuals, and compliance case histories that OSE has provided so abundantly. Small programs for civil rights technical assistance exist in other parts of the Department of

---

[10] Many of these documents are written and disseminated by the National Association of State Directors of Special Education, which depends to a large part on OSE grants. However, few SEA officials seemed aware of this linkage.

Education (e.g., the technical assistance centers established under
Title IV of the Civil Rights Act for desegregation and language minority
rights, and the Women's Educational Equity Act for Title IX). Funding
for these programs has generally been less than one-fourth the level
available under PL 94-142. It was eliminated entirely in President
Reagan's 1982 budget request but has been temporarily restored (at a
lower level) by the Congress.

Until recently, OCR has avoided providing any compliance advice
except in the context of complaint investigations and compliance
reviews. Many OCR officials fear that such advice, if based on
incomplete information about local conditions, could prove embarrassing
in later enforcement actions.[11] OCR investigative staff often urge
LEAs to request help from Title IV technical assistance centers; some
OCR "violation-corrected" letters document explicit agreements that the
local district will receive advice from assistance centers or advocacy
groups. Several of our OCR regional office respondents claimed that
technical assistance from such sources can often persuade local school
districts to make more extensive changes than could be obtained even
through successful enforcement actions. The effectiveness of Title IV
centers is in question, however, because many local school districts
have learned to doubt the legal correctness of their advice.

The reluctance of OCR field investigators to give compliance advice
is occasionally a source of tension. Local officials who cannot get
answers to their questions can charge OCR with playing a guessing game,
and with implicitly pressing the LEAs to provide beneficiary groups with
more than the law truly requires.[12] In partial response to this

_____

[11] This reluctance to give compliance advice is analogous to
dealings between representatives of the Internal Revenue Service and
taxpayers. IRS agents have given advice to taxpayers but have cautioned
that they are not legally accountable for their interpretations.

[12] OCR is not alone in perceiving this dilemma. The federal
managers of ESEA Title I have traditionally provided advice by letter
and telephone, but have occasionally been forced to reverse themselves
after conducting on-site monitoring visits. For Title I, the problem is
complicated by the fact that the Education Department Audit Agency
conducts its own compliance reviews, quite independent of Title I's
monitoring. The Audit Agency occasionally finds LEAs out of compliance
even after they have been cleared by Title I. Local and state officials
have complained bitterly to Congress about such inconsistent signals
from the federal government.

complaint, OCR established small Regional Technical Assistance Staffs
(RTAS) in 1980. Those staffs, composed of Section 504 compliance
experts, are meant to give more complete compliance advice than is
possible in the normal course of enforcement actions. To date, however,
the RTAS have limited themselves to Section 504 program accessibility
issues, and have provided only written materials and general workshops.
While on site, RTAS do not answer specific questions about the legality
of particular local practices.

Despite the establishment of the RTAS, OCR has not abandoned its
general reluctance to comment on local practices without a full
investigation. To date, however, the adoption of major technical
assistance efforts has been blocked by lack of funds for external grants
and OCR's general reluctance to give compliance advice.

Encouraging Beneficiary Organization

Many federal agencies try to extend their influence by creating
allies at local, state, and federal levels. OCR and OSE both extend
their influence by creating allies. Consistent with its general
strategy of influencing school districts indirectly through the actions
of others, OSE's efforts to encourage beneficiary organization are far
more complex and comprehensive than OCR's. Because OSE manages a major
grant program, it can provide funds to guarantee that SEAs and LEAs have
well-staffed special education offices (although OSE funds are probably
not identifiable as staff salaries at the local level, salaries are a
specifically allowable expense under PL 94-142). Staff of these
offices, it is assumed, can then act as local advocates for their own
programs.[13] Since OCR does not administer major grants programs, it

_____

[13] As our research makes clear, the assumption that state and
local special education staff will act as advocates for the Education
for All Handicapped Children program is a very good one. In the states
and school districts we visited, special education administrators were
long-time specialists in the education of the handicapped. Most had
started their careers as teachers for the handicapped or as college
professors of special education; several were either handicapped
themselves or had handicapped children in their families. Some were, of
course, more openly involved in advocacy than others. Many state
directors had directed lobbying in their state legislatures for
ambitious special education laws that predated PL 94-142. Local special

cannot hire its own local allies. Several of OCR's regulations require school districts to designate compliance coordinators; though some compliance coordinators act as advocates for the civil rights laws they administer, all are district-paid employees with multiple responsibilities. Few local compliance coordinators have the degree of specific professional training or the opportunities to advance in a well-established career line that is common among special education staff.[14]

Both OSE and OCR encourage the activities of beneficiary interest groups. However, OSE's efforts are far better funded and organized than OCR's. At the national, state, and particularly the local level, OSE sponsors both organizations of special education professionals and voluntary groups of parents of handicapped children. All of these groups are private membership organizations that receive funding from dues, donations, and other sources. OSE support comes through project grants tied to particular activities; however, without these grants, many of the organizations could not exist. Examples of the organizations and their OSE-funded activities include:

o   The National Association of State Directors of Special Education (NASDSE), which disseminates informal OSE policy documents, conducts training workshops, and sponsors national meetings between OSE staff and state directors.

---

education directors in the larger school districts also maintained contact with the state legislature: Two told us that they negotiated with state legislative committees, rather than their local school boards or state educational agencies, for their division's annual appropriations. Those local directors also saw themselves as leaders of local coalitions of teachers and parents of handicapped children. Special education directors in the smaller school districts were seldom as expressly political as those in the larger districts. However, they too almost invariably acted as strong advocates for special education programs and funds within the local educational bureaucracy.

[14] For results of a study on the activities and effectiveness of OCR-mandated compliance coordinators, see Paul T. Hill et al., Mechanisms for the Implementation of Civil Rights Guarantees by Educational Institutions, The Rand Corporation, R-2485-HEW, January 1980.

o   Local Parent Advocacy Coalitions,[15] which inform parents
     about their leverage on the writing of their children's
     individualized education plans, train parents for effective
     participation in due process hearings, and provide parent
     advocates or attorneys to help parents in disputes with local
     school district officials.[16]

OCR concentrates its limited funding on grants and contracts with a
small number of Washington-based national interest groups and a few
universities. OCR supports them only to conduct particular projects.
Funding is therefore transitory and focused on relatively narrow issues,
not general organization or advocacy. No group can rely on OCR
financial support for an extended period, and none receives enough money
from OCR to support advocacy efforts in a large number of states or
localities. Examples of OCR-supported activities include:

o   A grant to the National Organization for Women for a study of
     mediation as an alternative to complaint investigation.
o   Contracts with Hispanic-owned research groups to estimate the
     numbers of limited-English-speaking children in school
     districts that are not in compliance with guarantees for
     language minority students.[17]

---

[15] There are only 17 OSE-funded parent advocacy coalitions in the
U.S. However, their impact is much greater than this number would
suggest since they provide professional and moral support to many
unfunded groups throughout the country. At one such training session we
attended, two women traveled several hundred miles (at their own
expense) to get materials and ideas to improve their own fledgling--
and unfunded--parent advocacy group.

[16] A separate program funded under the Developmental Disabilities
Act of 1973 supplements OSE's efforts. That program funds "Protection
and Advocacy" law firms in states and territories. Like OSE's parent
advocacy coalitions, those groups provide legal representation and
counseling to parents.

[17] These guarantees emerged from Lau v. Nichols, 414 U.S. 563,
1974.

o   A contract with a private consulting firm to provide technical
    assistance to universities on retaining black students.

Few, if any, of these activities have directly assisted in the
formation or maintenance of local interest groups. To the extent that
any such assistance has come from Washington, it has been initiated by
the interest groups themselves and funded by donations or foundation
grants. Examples include national analysis and advocacy done by the
Children's Defense Fund and the local organizational work done by the
National Organization for Women, all with foundation funding.

OCR has never treated major funding for assistance to interest
groups (or for R&D activities that could assist such groups) as a high
priority. Though OCR's total appropriations have grown from $16 to $54
million in the period 1975-1980,[18] its budget for external grants and
contracts has not grown over that period at all.[19] OCR clearly
prefers to rely on its traditional strategy of using federal employees
to negotiate compliance agreements in the course of complaint
investigations and compliance reviews.

Creating Leverage for Beneficiaries and Advocates

This form of leverage is distinct from encouraging beneficiary
organizations. Once interest groups are established, they may or may
not have ready access to local decision processes. Federal agencies can
increase beneficiary groups' leverage by requiring local governments to
consult with beneficiary groups by providing beneficiaries with special
access to courts or quasi-judicial forums, or by giving beneficiary
groups the power to approve or disapprove how federal grants are used.
At a minimum, these arrangements ensure that beneficiaries' views will
be considered. Politically sophisticated and well-organized interest
groups can use such leverage to influence a broad range of decisions.

_____

[18] The figures in the text refer only to OCR's education
activities; that is, we have deleted OCR's appropriations for activities
other than education when the agency was in the U.S. Department of
Health, Education, and Welfare.
[19] Last year the agency requested an increased technical
assistance budget, but this was turned down by the Secretary of
Education.

Both OCR and OSE make some efforts to create leverage for local beneficiaries and advocates. OSE's efforts are particularly vigorous. It invests great energy to ensure that the statutory requirements are in place and operating for individualized education programs and due process procedures. These instruments give parents enormous leverage over the delivery of services to their children. Coalitions of parents can also raise broader issues of special education policy through the hearing process and subsequent appeals to the courts. The availability of these routes of appeal strengthens parents' hands in all sorts of informal negotiations. School administrators who are tempted to ignore parents' views in the formulation of individualized education plans know that parents can initiate time-consuming due process hearings and may also be upheld by the hearing officer. School board members and superintendents are reluctant to oppose groups that are well organized and have ready access to the courts.[20]

The individualized education plan and the due process system also confer leverage on special education professionals. Given the vagueness of PL 94-142's service standard (free appropriate public education for every handicapped child), expert judgments about children's needs are highly influential. At a minimum, no school district can offer a handicapped child less service than its own special education staff thinks is appropriate. Should district-employed experts lower their standards under pressure from their superiors, parents can obtain countervailing testimony from independent experts. This means that the professional standards of special education experts--psychologists, social workers, child care workers, nurses, and physicians--establish threshold levels of service quality.

_____

[20] Though there are no national data on the outcomes of due process hearings, evidence from a few states and localities indicates that parents prevail in between one-third and one-half of all PL 94-142 complaints that are decided by a hearing officer or judge. In an individual case, the parents' chance of prevailing depends on the issue involved, the performance of witnesses and counsel, and other local factors. In general, however, school officials must assume that parents who initiate complaints have a good chance of winning. See Kirst and Bertken, op. cit.; and Peter Kuriloff et al., When Handicapped Children Go to Court: Assessing the Impact of Legal Reform of Special Education in Pennsylvania, Project No. Neg.-003-0192, Project on Student

Consistent with the low priority it attaches to indirect methods of influence, OCR has not made major efforts to create beneficiary leverage. OCR's regulations for Title IX and Section 504 require school districts to conduct one-time self-evaluations of their compliance status and to establish local grievance procedures. These processes now make real but minor contributions to local beneficiaries' leverage.[21]

We expected that our fieldwork would show that local beneficiaries used the threat of a complaint to OCR as a source of leverage in bargaining with school officials. However, we found that the threat of an OCR investigation was seldom an important bargaining resource. In addition, potential complainants seldom understand the law or OCR's mission well enough to formulate the issues effectively.[22] Their complaints frequently raised issues that were outside OCR's jurisdiction (about 40 percent of all complaints to OCR are closed without investigation for these reasons) or requested remedies that OCR had no power to provide. Many complainants make no effort to resolve their problems locally before contacting OCR. Most of the school district respondents with whom we discussed particular complaints claimed that the first information about the complaint came from OCR, not the complainant. OCR regional office personnel estimate that nearly 25 percent of the complainants contact OCR without first warning school officials.

Classification and the Law, National Institute of Education, Washington, D.C., 1979.

[21] Hill et al., op. cit., concluded that beneficiaries and their advocates have, on occasion, been able to use the self-evaluation process to create significant local compliance agendas. Likewise, many local officials are willing to grant beneficiaries' requests rather than subject themselves to the inconvenience and possible embarrassment of a formal hearing. With relatively minor changes in requirements--e.g., periodic renewals of self-evaluations, publication of results, and greater publicity about the existence of the grievance processes--these sources of leverage could become somewhat more important. But without major changes, such as giving beneficiaries standing to sue over inadequate self-evaluation grievance processes, these sources of leverage could never approach the power of those established under PL 94-142.

[22] OCR's jurisdiction and authority are not unlimited. It cannot be a source of relief for complainants simply seeking revenge on local officials, nor can it force people to change their attitudes and beliefs. We encountered instances in our fieldwork where a parent or individual had a grievance that fit within OCR's mandate but did not know (and was not told) how to submit an appropriate complaint.

A few sophisticated interest groups, especially the NAACP, were able to use the threat of complaint to OCR effectively. Local officials know that those groups understand the law well enough to formulate a complaint that has face validity, and know OCR procedures well enough to provide the background for a serious investigation. The threat of an OCR investigation is always implicit in those groups' bargaining with school officials.

In general, the threat of OCR's complaint investigation has seldom become an effective tool in the hands of local advocates. Compared with the locally administered PL 94-142 individualized education plan and due process requirements, OCR's centrally administered complaint process does little to encourage or strengthen local beneficiaries' efforts on their own behalf.

Individual Sanctions

Individual rewards and sanctions differ from the corporate rewards and sanctions discussed above; they affect the income, satisfaction, and career prospects of _individual_ public officials. Adverse personal publicity, bad performance ratings, and firing are all examples of individual sanctions; promotion, praise, training opportunities, and pay raises are all examples of individual rewards.[23]

Neither OSE nor OCR directly manipulates individual sanctions. Neither agency hires, fires, or promotes local school administrators. However, actions by the two federal agencies can stimulate local events that affect administrators' careers. The effects of federal actions are indirect and are mediated by the reactions of local beneficiary groups, newspapers, and school officials, but the effects are real. Local administrators are keenly aware of personal costs of fighting with

---

[23] The distinction between corporate and individual sanction is murky when, for example, an official is fired after his organization is penalized for noncompliance. The distinction is clear, however, when individual careers are affected in the absence of corporate sanctions. For example, even while working successfully to avoid an official finding of noncompliance, individual officials can suffer adverse publicity, have their schedules preempted by enforcement actions and litigation, and lose control of the day-to-day activities they are supposed to supervise.

federal agencies, and are therefore eager to conclude any business with OSE and OCR as quickly and smoothly as possible. Examples of the individual sanctions that are implicitly threatened by any interaction with OSE and OCR include:

Controversy. Officials who are charged with improper administration of federal funds or denial of civil rights often find their relationships with beneficiary groups seriously strained. Such strains often persist even after the original charges are dropped or proved false. Even if the local school district is eventually found in compliance, it is likely that some local people will continue to believe or suspect that the official is not fair or competent. Knowing this, OCR field investigators occasionally either encourage complainants to seek publicity or make contacts with local newspapers themselves. Such publicity, often in stories headed "School district may lose federal funds due to maladministration," calls public attention to the local official's intransigence.

OSE has sought publicity for a few of its battles with SEAs. At the local level, parent advocacy centers and other OSE-supported beneficiary groups routinely use the news media to publicize their grievances.

Suspension of the Assumption of Competence. No official can operate without some range of discretion based on deference for his expertise. Merely having a federal agency come into a local school district casts doubt on an official's competence. Enforcement actions and judicial hearings suspend deference to the official's judgment and force minute examination of his or her actions. Such processes can bring to light small errors that may never have been detected and raise the possibility that the official will never regain the deference he or she had enjoyed in the past.

Most local officials we interviewed had dealt with OCR or PL 94-142 disputes without any such ill effects. Perhaps to avoid adversity, some top-level local officials delegate responsibility for dealing with OCR to their subordinates. When this occurs they send an implicit message that matters should henceforth be dealt with smoothly, i.e., that top officials should not be troubled further. This creates an incentive for the lower-level officials to reach a negotiated settlement with OCR.

However, we encountered a small number of officials whose dealings with OCR investigations or PL 94-142 disputes had blighted their careers. One state special education director we interviewed was resigning because a complaint had revealed his office's systematic failures to rectify known cases of local noncompliance. An assistant superintendent in a large LEA in another state was demoted to a minor bureaucratic post after a mistake in his dealings with OCR led to a long delay in approval of the district's ESAA grant.

Even when local officials suffer no tangible harm, many feel robbed of the satisfaction they seek from their jobs. As one special education administrator told us, "I think of myself as someone who wants to help these little kids, and I think I'm good at it. I hate it when people poke around trying to show that I was uncaring or did something wrong." Consequently, most officials deal with disputes over civil rights and the handicapped as if they posed present dangers to their careers.

Loss of Control Over Working Time. To respond to enforcement actions, local officials must set aside at least part of their normal duties.[24] For many officials, this represents a potential threat to their career goals. At a minimum, it means that activities for which they are normally responsible may be poorly done, and their records blemished accordingly. For higher officials--especially superintendents and people aspiring to be superintendents--loss of control over working time may cripple projects on which they had pinned their hopes for job security or advancement. Likewise, administrators who are assigned as part-time compliance coordinators for unfunded requirements like Title IX and Section 504 can definitely suffer from the time demands of federal requirements.[25]

Such individual sanctions do not always work. Some local administrators are able to turn some of the sanctions, especially

---

[24] We found at least one official who was clever and powerful enough to shift these burdens to his subordinates, who then lost control over their working time. This official never negotiated with OCR to reduce data requests or investigation efforts. The subordinates deeply resented the federal intrusion, not realizing that their supervisor was using them so he could present a "good guy" image to OCR.

[25] See Hill et al., op. cit., about the lack of career rewards for local Title IX and Section 504 coordinators.

adverse publicity and controversy, to their own advantage by portraying federal officials as outside meddlers or program requirements as unreasonable, and themselves as defenders of local autonomy. Administrators in very conservative communities can occasionally feel comfortable taking such a course. Most of our respondents, however, considered that an extremely risky factor, and preferred to avoid the personal risks of opposing OCR- or OSE-supported advocates whenever possible.

Individual Rewards

Federal agencies can create individual rewards for local administrators who promote local compliance activities or cooperate with federal officials. Such rewards are seldom obvious direct payments for services rendered. They are activities that enhance administrators' career opportunities or their status within their own school systems.

OCR is able to offer few such rewards. It does not subsidize training programs or prizes, and there is no obvious civil rights "career ladder" (i.e., a succession of positions in school districts, state government, or federal government) up which professional civil rights compliance specialists can hope to advance.[26]

OSE creates many individual rewards for special education administrators. Since before the enactment of PL 94-142, OSE has consciously nurtured the development of the special education profession. Now special education is an important academic discipline that offers many career opportunities in research and teaching, as well as a clinical and administrative career ladder that unites teachers, school principals, LEA and SEA administrators, and federal employees. OSE helps maintain schools of education, funds research, subsidizes college undergraduate and graduate students, and helps pay the salaries of administrators at all levels.[27] It also encourages professional

---

[26] There may be such a career ladder in higher education--from state or federal educational opportunity specialist to full-time civil rights coordinator in a college or university, to employment as an OCR regional director or Washington office manager. But no such career succession is evident on the elementary and secondary level. See Hill et al., op. cit., Chap. 3, for a discussion of career incentives for civil rights coordinators in higher education.

[27] PL 94-142 also helps create career opportunities for another group of professionals, viz., the small number of attorneys who

meetings that reinforce individuals' career identities and provides opportunities for personal recognition. There are, consequently, important individual rewards for local educators.

The effects of these individual rewards are pervasive. Though the special education profession existed before OSE, it is a cohesive, strong source of local allies for PL 94-142 programs largely because of OSE's consistent and generous nurturance.

DIFFERENT MODELS OF FEDERAL INFLUENCE

As the preceding shows, the two agencies use all of the influence methods, but in different ways and with different degrees of emphasis. Table 3 summarizes the differences in the two agencies' reliance on the various influence mechanisms.

Table 3

COMPARISON OF OCR'S AND OSE'S USE OF INFLUENCE METHODS

	Importance of Method	
Method	OCR	OSE
Threat of corporate penalties	Secondary	Slight
Individual sanctions	Secondary	Slight
Process costs	Primary	Slight
Corporate rewards	Slight	Secondary
Individual rewards	Slight	Primary
Technical assistance	Slight	Primary
Beneficiary organizations	Slight	Primary
Beneficiary leverage	Slight	Primary

Table 3 makes evident several facts that were implicit in the preceding discussion. First, OSE makes significant use of a broader range of influence mechanisms than does OCR. Second, OCR relies

---

specialize in representing parents. Though handicapped law is apparently not a highly lucrative specialty, it creates enough business to encourage some law schools to offer related courses. OSE subsidizes some of these courses, and also pays for the training of lay advocates (see "Creating Beneficiary Leverage," above).

primarily on mechanisms that require direct federal involvement
in monitoring local activities and imposing costs and penalties. The
threat of corporate penalties, process costs, and individual sanctions
are OCR's primary mechanisms of influence; they are all directly
operated by federal officials--field investigators, regional directors,
and headquarters personnel--who negotiate directly with local school
officials. Third, in contrast, OSE relies primarily on mechanisms that
rely on the self-interested actions of local individuals, particularly
special education professionals and parents of handicapped children.
OSE provides a system of individual rewards and technical assistance to
motivate and guide local professionals, and provides resources for
beneficiary groups to organize and act on their own. These differences
reflect the two organizations' histories and philosophies. They
represent two very different basic models of federal influence: The
first, reflecting OCR's dominant mode of influence, is enforcement; the
second, reflecting OSE's emphasis, is promotion. The rest of this
section will define the two models and explain their basic assumptions
and limitations.

Enforcement

Most regulatory systems, including OCR's, are based on an economic
model of enforcement developed to explain the regulation of private
firms.[28] The model is easiest to explain in terms of profit-making
businesses: It assumes that firms violate specific legal requirements
(e.g., antipollution laws) because it is more profitable to do so.
Maintaining existing practices (e.g., continuing to use toxic chemicals
or to discharge pollutants) is cheaper than changing those practices.
Enforcement works by making noncompliance less profitable than
compliance.

To deter noncompliance, regulatory agencies must make regulated
firms believe that there is a finite probability of being found in
violation, and that penalties are certain once noncompliance is

_____

[28] For an excellent general discussion of enforcement theory, see
W. Kip Viscusi and Richard J. Zeckhauser, "Optional Standards with
Incomplete Enforcement," Public Policy, Vol. 27, Fall 1979, pp. 437-456.

detected. For firms, noncompliance is a rational strategy unless the expected value of the fine (i.e., the likelihood of detection multiplied by the actual fine) is greater than or equal to the costs to the firm of changing its activities to come into compliance. Smaller penalties may induce compliance if firms are averse to risk or if they also take account of intangible costs, such as bad publicity. In addition, the costs of fact-finding, negotiation, and litigation can be significant, and effectively increase the value of fines paid by violators.[29]

This model makes explicit the assumptions behind OCR's use of corporate penalties and process costs.[30] OCR identifies instances of noncompliance, either through compliance reviews or complaint investigation, and can impose sanctions to punish violators. School districts take account of the frequency and accuracy of federal monitoring efforts and the likelihood that OCR can impose a penalty if it tries to do so. They also consider the intangible costs, such as bad publicity and the stress of dealing with OCR.

Some important differences between school districts and private business firms complicate the problem of enforcement. For example:

---

[29] Such process costs are two-edged swords, however. Enforcement agencies must also pay such costs, and high process costs might force them to reduce the level of their monitoring efforts. In addition, regulated firms must bear process costs whenever they are charged with a violation, whether they are guilty or not. If a substantial fraction of the firms charged with violations are eventually found not guilty, the connection between process costs and other penalties is attenuated; process costs therefore accrue to the regulated industry, not specifically to the violators.

[30] The economic model does not expressly consider individual sanctions. A very similar model could, however, explain their operation. In the absence of any incentives to change their current courses of action, individual local officials will continue habitually discriminatory practices. Individual sanctions increase the personal cost of discriminating, so that changing a habitual discriminatory practice is less personally stressful than continuing it. Therefore, individual local officials may stop discriminating even when they know that corporate penalties are unlikely. Unfortunately, the enforcement model is very difficult to operationalize at the individual level, since all costs and benefits are subjective. The essential logic holds, however.

o Because school districts are not in business to make a profit, their financial gains from conducting noncompliant programs are hard to estimate. It is therefore difficult for OCR to determine what kind of or how large a penalty should be imposed, or for a school district to estimate what costs it is likely to have to pay.[31]

o Because school districts do not operate in a highly competitive market, severe sanctions are not likely to put violators out of business.

o Because school districts do not charge for their services, the costs of compliance (or of penalties) cannot be passed on directly to consumers. Public agencies can, in theory, raise taxes, but many LEAs are at the limit of their taxing authority and can pay compliance costs only by reducing other services.

For these reasons, it is virtually impossible for OCR to calibrate its fines or other sanctions exactly.[32]

Nonetheless, OCR's enforcement actions significantly affect many school districts. School officials dread adverse publicity and have limited time and money to devote to negotiation and litigation. Even when noncompliance is hard to define and penalties cannot be imposed with precision, school districts are clearly willing to concede a good deal to avoid the process costs, individual sanctions, and penalties that OCR enforcement actions can create.

---

[31] These "penalties" and "costs" include all the components of the enforcement model: corporate penalties, individual sanctions, and process costs.

[32] Even if sanctions could be precisely calibrated, enforcement officials seldom have much influence over the levels of penalties imposed. Political intervention by state, local, and Congressional officials elevates these decisions at least to the Secretary's level; penalties are regularly reduced to mere tokens by that process. That fact, however, does not distinguish education from other areas of regulation.

Promotion

Promotion is a more subtle and diffuse influence strategy. Because it is difficult to reduce to a simple model, it has not been systematically formulated by social scientists. But promotion is a very effective--and possibly the dominant--mode of intergovernmental influence in our federal system.

The essence of promotion is encouragement and assistance to local entities who will act in their own interests to promote federal policy goals. The classic example of a federal promotion strategy is the Agricultural Extension Service. Federal officials and local farmers share the goal of increasing agricultural productivity; USDA extension agents provide information about new techniques, and farmers adopt the techniques on their own initiative.

Not all promotional activities can be as simple and direct as Agricultural Extension. Local actors may not acknowledge the federal government's competence to give technical advice (as was the case with federal efforts to promote the adoption of household energy-saving devices), or be willing to adopt federal priorities (as had been the case with affirmative action requirements). As shown in a study of Swedish occupational safety and health programs, promotion can be effective even when priorities are in dispute.[33] Promotion can work whenever cultural norms favor negotiation among affected groups and when a well-established local group, however small, is willing to act in support of federal program beneficiaries. Any influence strategy that relies on the actions of local people must therefore encourage (and in some instances create) local factions that are naturally sympathetic with federal program goals.

Creating a federal promotional strategy in education is not a simple matter. The federal government typically has neither the technical expertise nor political legitimacy to intervene openly in local affairs. Local educators hotly resist any federal prescriptiveness about instructional processes, and local communities

_____

[33] Steven Kelman, Regulating America, Regulating Sweden: A Comparative Study of Occupational Safety and Health Policy, The MIT Press, Cambridge, Massachusetts, 1981.

tend to be divided about how much special treatment for minority groups is desirable.

As OSE's experience shows, however, local reluctance to adopt federal priorities does not rule out a promotional strategy. OSE's promotional strategy uses a wide array of sources of local support. As the preceding subsection demonstrated, OSE has created and nurtured a whole profession, affected public attitudes, provided authoritative technical advice, helped organize beneficiary groups, and created channels through which local special education supporters can assert their demands. Furthermore, OSE has been able to foster these promotional activities through its fairly rigorous monitoring and enforcement efforts at the state level.

Promotion is not without its drawbacks. Advocates for special education are better organized and more skillful in some localities than in others; some school boards resent the financial demands imposed by PL 94-142 guarantees; and some communities have vocal opposition groups. OSE's critics (e.g., the Education Advocates Coalition previously discussed) point to the limitations of the promotional strategy, and demand a greater emphasis on enforcement at the local level. They argue, in effect, that the promotional strategy gets adequate education for handicapped children who live in law-abiding school districts and whose parents are sophisticated and active. But it does not protect children whose parents are uninformed or passive, or who face determined opposition from school officials.

CONCLUSION

Since the passage of the Elementary and Secondary Education Act's Title I in 1965, much of the debate about the administration of federal education programs has concerned the choice between the enforcement and promotional strategies. Scandals about misuses of federal funds and charges of ignoring federal intent create demands for rigorous enforcement,[34] and local superintendents and school board members

---

[34] At least three such "scandals" have led to significant increases in enforcement activity. A report on misuses of Title I funds produced enormous increases in federal monitoring and auditing (Ruby Martin and Phyllis McClure, Title I of ESEA: Is It Helping Poor Children?, Washington Research Project of the Southern Center for

continually demand "more help and less bullying" from the federal government.[35] As a result, all federal education programs, OCR and OSE included, use combinations of enforcement and promotion.

The debate swings back and forth between advocates and opponents of the two strategies. Most participants in the debate implicitly recognize that both enforcement and promotion have strengths and weaknesses, and that some situations require more of one strategy and less of the other. But there has been little systematic effort either to assess the two strategies' effectiveness or to identify their respective best uses. Section IV lays the groundwork for such an assessment by presenting results of our research on school districts' responses to OCR's and OSE's efforts to influence them.

Studies in Public Policy and the National Association for the Advancement of Colored People Legal Defense and Educational Fund, Washington, D.C., 1970). The plaintiffs in Adams v. Richardson claimed that several states were maintaining racially discriminatory dual systems of higher education, and the resulting court order required OCR to increase significantly its allocation of staff for complaint resolution. The Education Advocates Coalition report, op. cit., alleged widespread noncompliance with PL 94-142, and led OSE both to increase its own monitoring efforts and to include OCR staff in its reviews of state plans, routine monitoring, and complaint resolutions.

[35] See, for example, Hearings Before the Subcommittee on Elementary, Secondary, and Vocational Education of the Committee on Education and Labor, House of Representatives, 95th Cong., 1st sess., on H.R. 15, Parts 16-18, 1977.

IV. RESULTS OF FEDERAL INFLUENCE EFFORTS

Section III explained how OCR and OSE try to influence school
districts. This section examines the responses of SEAs and LEAs to
those efforts. The specific responses we examine include:

o   Changes in SEA and LEA decisionmaking processes;
o   Changes in specific educational or administrative processes;
    and
o   Changes in general policies.

The discussion is organized around the two basic influence
strategies identified at the end of Sec. III: enforcement and
promotion. It reports our findings about typical state and local
responses, first to federal enforcement efforts, and second to
promotional activities. It then briefly mentions beneficiary responses
to the two strategies. Because OCR makes the most assiduous use of
enforcement, most of the discussion of that strategy will focus on OCR;
correspondingly, most of the discussion of promotion will focus on OSE.

ENFORCEMENT

Effects on Decisionmaking Processes

In the school districts we visited, we found a remarkably
consistent set of responses to OCR enforcement actions. According to
local officials, districts' responses to OCR mature and stabilize over
time. After a panicky and highly disruptive reaction to the first OCR
compliance review or complaint investigation, most districts develop
orderly procedures both for dealing with OCR and implementing any
required policy changes.

Accounts of districts' first contacts with OCR are uniformly
dramatic. District officials feel threatened by OCR's inquiries, afraid
that they might become victims of "witch hunting." OCR's initial
contact--which usually comes in the form of a stiff, legalistically
worded request for detailed information about the district practices to

be investigated--often makes local officials think that OCR enters an investigation assuming that a violation exists. In addition, many local officials have an exaggerated image of the penalties that OCR is likely to impose. In our interviews, some even discussed the possible consequences of an OCR investigation in such terms as "going to jail." These concerns pervade the school district's administrative staff. Preparations for a district's first OCR visit typically involve members of the school board, the superintendent, heads and members of most central office staff units, and principals and teachers in all schools that could possibly attract OCR investigators' attention.

This "crisis" response is exactly what we expected to find. Before undertaking the fieldwork, we conducted informal conversations with state school board members and local superintendents who told us of the enormous disruptions caused by OCR site visits. However, we were surprised to find that such disruptions are one-time events. After their first experience with enforcement, local officials gain a more moderate view of OCR's intent and capacity, and develop bureaucratic channels for the routine processing of future investigations. Most subsequent OCR investigations are seen as minor problems to be handled routinely by specialized units in the central office staff. School board members, principals, and teachers are seldom involved.[1]

---

[1] Local officials clearly have an incentive to continue portraying civil rights enforcement as a highly stressful and disruptive phenomenon. The public perception of OCR as a rough and unscrupulous investigative agency threatens OCR's political support. Congress, in particular, cannot support a federal agency that bullies local public officials. OCR site reviewers therefore are under pressure to prove their reasonableness and moderation; local officials can easily find allies to support them against OCR investigators who exceed their legal authority or bargain harshly.

Our fieldwork revealed so few abuses of OCR's authority that we were forced to ask where the stories and stereotypes came from. Local officials and OCR staff both agreed that OCR was far more aggressive in the early negotiations over school desegregation than they were now. Stories of recent abuses are few and far between, but most are widely known and frequently repeated. Though few local officials could cite any problems from their own experience, many knew about two 1978 Title IX actions, one opposing father-son banquets and another opposing local dress codes. Local officials have good political reasons for keeping such stories alive. But, as we learned, widely accepted stereotypes are bad sources of evidence about actual agency performance.

The bureaucratization of LEA response is consistent with organizational theory. As Thompson argues, organizations seek to buffer their "technical cores" from the effects of new pressures by establishing special administrative units.[2] Meyer applied the theory to school districts.[3] When school districts come under external pressure (e.g., from regulatory agencies or courts), they protect their "technical cores"--schools and classrooms--by creating new central office units charged with responsibility for compliance. These units answer any requests from regulatory agencies and courts, and try to deflect any efforts to change school or classroom activities. Such units transform potentially disruptive demands into routine bureaucratic work. Responses to new demands (whether from parents, school board politicians, or state and federal regulators) are purely procedural: New records are kept, reports filed, officials appointed, and administrative units established. Changes filter down to the schools slowly and in the most limited form possible.

OCR can take advantage of a local school district's initial inexperience and anxiety. Investigators can push for compliance with more vigor knowing the district will acquiesce to avoid further troubles, real or imagined. Many districts appear more willing to make concessions to OCR on their first encounter than later. The number and degree of those concessions, however, is limited by two factors. The first is the district's unwillingness to change procedures that they think are "right" educationally. One district we visited dug in its heels when staff believed a "trainable mentally retarded" student was better served in a special facility than in a neighborhood school. It was for the best interests of the child, they argued, and they would not accede to the parents' preference to have the child declared "educable

---

[2] James D. Thompson, Organizations in Action, McGraw-Hill, New York, 1967.

[3] John W. Meyer, The Impact of the Centralization of Educational Funding and Control on State and Local Organizational Governance, Program Report No. 79-B20, Stanford University, August 1979; and John W. Meyer et al., Institutional and Technical Sources of Organizational Structure Explaining the Structure of Educational Organizations, Project Report No. 79-A9, Stanford University, May 1980.

mentally retarded." The second factor that limits a district's willingness to make concessions is the presence of a lawyer on the district's side. Some districts have obtained legal counsel even before their first brush with OCR (usually as a result of contacts with other federal enforcement agencies). Those districts rely on the lawyer to define their rights and obligations and are unlikely to make concessions merely to appease OCR.

The "crisis" response described above is a natural part of the district's learning process. Immediately after the first "crisis," the LEA organizes a much tighter and more orderly response system. The details of the subsequent organizational response vary. In the larger districts (generally those with over 25,000 student population), responsibility for contacts with OCR was delegated to federal program specialists.[4] Those specialists were responsible for analyzing communications from OCR, obtaining any requested information, planning and managing district cooperation with site visits, and supervising the implementation of any negotiated policy changes. They could become deeply involved in particular investigations, and some were keenly aware of the potential individual sanctions and effects on local practices that OCR's actions could create. But the stress of dealing with enforcement officials was usually limited to these few specialists. School board members were often not informed about fact-finding and negotiation efforts;[5] superintendents were rarely participants except to greet the OCR team; and school principals and teachers were seldom affected, except insofar as limited specific changes in their practices were required by a negotiated settlement.

---

[4] Such specialists are often difficult for outsiders to find. Their role is internal to the educational bureaucracy and they often have very low public profiles. Their titles are not descriptive, e.g., "compliance officer," "federal programs coordinator," or "assistant superintendent." To find such officials for our fieldwork, we found it most efficient to ask for the special education director, whom we then queried for the names of relevant people. We can only speculate on the difficulties a complainant encounters when trying to find these officials in order to lodge a grievance with the local school system.

[5] In most instances, school board members learned of enforcement actions indirectly through press reports or representations by complainants during board meetings.

Few of the smaller districts could afford the luxury of a full-time compliance specialist. In most such districts, however, the superintendent or a deputy became the de facto compliance specialist. Again, those officials quickly learned how to deal with OCR in a routine fashion, without perturbing school board politics or the schools.

Several districts, both large and small, also retained local private attorneys to counsel and represent them after their first contacts with OCR. The attorney usually provided straightforward legal advice, e.g., on the limits of OCR's mission and authority and about the LEA's apparent obligations under federal statutes and regulations. Attorneys in some districts also gave tactical advice, and some drafted responses to OCR's letters and conducted negotiations personally. In larger districts with full-time compliance coordinators, the attorney's role varied from case to case, depending on the legal and political complexity of the problems involved. Attorneys can make matters very difficult for OCR by, for example, citing case law questioning the agency's authority,[6] and counseling local school district staff with regard to their obligation to provide data (e.g., advising the school district to claim that the data requested are covered by confidentiality rules). Some investigators appear to relish these sorts of encounters; others prefer to avoid them whenever possible.

Once responsibility for enforcement-related work is delegated, problems seldom come to the attention of the superintendent or school board members. Top officials become involved only if negotiations break down, or if the OCR regional office threatens to send the case to Washington for enforcement. In normal circumstances, OCR's influence works through bureaucratic processes at the middle level of school district administration, rather than through overt pressures on the school board or superintendent. The next subsection discusses the substantive effects of these processes, i.e., the ways that school districts change their policies in response to OCR enforcement.

---

[6] One example concerns the scope of OCR's jurisdiction. Some federal courts have ruled that, so long as a school or its students receives federal funds, OCR may investigate any alleged violation. Other courts have restricted OCR's purview to complaints related to programs directly supported by federal funds. OCR regional offices are forced to follow different practices, depending on what jurisdiction they are in.

Effects on Substantive Policy and Practice

In our interviews with local officials, we probed deeply for evidence about whether LEAs make any real changes in response to OCR's enforcement activities. What we learned can be summarized in three simple points:

o   OCR investigations, negotiations, and sanctions definitely can produce change at the local level.

o   The changes produced are limited in scope. Complaint resolution and compliance reviews can change the LEA's treatment of a particular individual (the complainant) or a particular group, or produce a change in administrative practices (e.g., establishing grievance procedures), but it has little effect on the school district's general orientation toward disadvantaged groups.

o   LEAs apparently make the changes that they expressly and unambiguously promise, but take advantage of any ambiguities in their agreement with OCR.

To expand on the three points:

Changes Made. OCR compliance reviews and complaint investigations create changes at the local level in two ways: First, some LEAs eliminate discriminatory practices immediately upon hearing that an OCR investigation is imminent. A few of our district respondents welcomed OCR intervention because it gave them the leverage necessary to effect changes they had wanted for some time. Second, once an OCR investigation is complete and a district is found in violation of the law, the vast majority of LEAs agree to change specific practices in order to avoid formal charges of noncompliance and the rigors of administrative hearings.

Based on the testimony of local officials, it is clear that OCR's influence mechanisms, especially process costs, usually work as intended. The enforcement process does increase the cost of noncompliance. Enforcement can call attention to problems that have been neglected and encourage a slight but real change in priorities.

When, as may be the case, discriminatory local practices are based more on habit and neglect than on strongly held local preferences, enforcement provides the impetus for change.[7]

Changes Are Limited. As the preceding paragraphs make clear, enforcement actions produce changes because the changes demanded are usually limited and only mildly controversial. Changes due to enforcement in the districts we visited include:

o Rehiring a handicapped teacher whose unfavorable performance ratings were probably not negative enough to get a nonhandicapped person fired;

o Establishing a girl's softball league in the current school year rather than in the next school year, as initially planned;

o Naming a Title IX compliance officer;

o Establishing procedures to evacuate mobility-impaired students in the event of an emergency;

o Providing an interpreter for a deaf child who had previously had to rely on lip-reading and the teacher's writing on the blackboard;

o "Mainstreaming" handicapped students two years ahead of the district's plan to do such; and

o Increasing the teacher:student ratio in a self-contained special education class.

---

[7] These findings reflect the realities of the early 1980s. Had we conducted similar research in the late 1960s, when OCR was aggressively enforcing the laws against school segregation, our findings might have been very different. Local resistance to desegregation was based on strongly held values and both OCR and the courts were willing to impose major corporate sanctions. In those times, enforcement may have succeeded less often than now, but created far greater changes when it worked. Today, however, OCR's workload involves few such fundamental conflicts of values. Even those cases on racial discrimination involve issues that are far more subtle than the maintenance of dual school systems. Our findings clearly reflect the nature of today's issues, which appear to be cooler, more subtle, and more susceptible to resolution through application of mild incentives than were the early desegregation issues.

Such changes are important to the individual students and teachers involved, but nearly all the changes are very narrow in scope. Most of the changes we saw affected administrative procedures (e.g., adoption of nondiscrimination assurances) or simply accelerated policy changes that the district was already making. Few corrective actions reflected fundamental changes in a district's orientation toward a whole disadvantaged group. When deaf children were assigned interpreters, it did not necessarily follow that these same students received other benefits or related services. A complaint that too many black children were erroneously classified as mentally retarded did not stimulate a broad effort to protect blacks from other stigmatizing labels. The substantive changes we saw were specific, discrete, and frequently affected only those individuals directly involved in the enforcement process. These facts certainly reinforce OCR officials' belief, reported in Sec. II, that noncompliance is nearly universal, even after compliance agreements are implemented.

OCR's intent in resolving complaints is to create broad changes in district policy. That is why OCR insists on obtaining general pledges of nondiscrimination. But OCR does not or cannot monitor the day-to-day implementation of such general pledges, and we found little substantive change as a result of districts' assurances that they will not discriminate.

One important exception to these generalizations was evident in the districts we visited. OCR enforcement had stimulated broad changes in many districts' services to language minority students. OCR created those changes through its enforcement of the Supreme Court's decree in Lau v. Nichols. The broad success of that effort can be attributed to a number of factors that are inevitably absent from most enforcement actions. The factors include:

o   A clear statutory mandate, based on the Supreme Court's widely publicized interpretation of Title VI of the 1964 Civil Rights Act;

o   Community acceptance of a decree from the U.S. Supreme Court
    that OCR is implementing;

o   A concrete and widely publicized set of compliance criteria,
    the "Lau guarantees," which were established by a task force of
    linguistic experts assembled by OCR;

o   Widespread awareness among school officials that many language
    minority students were not getting adequate services in school;

o   The special leverage available to OCR through the Emergency
    School Aid Act pregrant review process. Since most language
    minority students were concentrated in local school districts
    that also had desegregation plans, OCR's actions raised the
    threat of very important corporate sanctions against the school
    districts.

OCR's efforts were also reinforced by two independent sources of
pressure:

o   The ever-present prospect of lawsuits against individual school
    districts, brought by national Hispanic advocacy groups;

o   Local language and speech directors' support for the change.
    Those professionals knew that compliance with the Lau
    guarantees would inevitably increase the number of students
    served, staff, budget, and organizational status of local
    bilingual education administrators' responsibilities.

In combination, these factors created broad changes in LEA policy.
The general shortage of education funding and ambiguities about future
federal intent caused by Secretary Bell's withdrawal of the proposed Lau
regulations have slowed the implementation of recent compliance
agreements. But both OCR and local school district staff agree that Lau
compliance agreements have provided agendas for real change in a great
many school districts.

The factors that contributed to the success of OCR's Lau
enforcement are missing from the vast majority of its compliance reviews
and complaint investigations. Given the Reagan Administration's

reluctance to undertake major compliance reviews and impose corporate
sanctions, the more modest changes reported above will probably continue
to be the typical outcomes of OCR's enforcement efforts.

Local School Districts Make the Specific Changes They Promise.
Local officials claimed to have made all of the changes that were
unambiguously required by their compliance agreements with OCR. We were
unable to verify all of those claims directly, of course. However, as
the preceding section shows, most of the required changes were so
concrete and limited in scope that the LEAs had no incentive not to make
them. In the normal course of negotiations, it is the school district,
not OCR, that formulates the remedial plan. Local officials know what
changes are possible, and generally need not promise anything that
exceeds their financial or technical resources. OCR often presses for
more ambitious changes than local districts think they can afford; the
two sides usually compromise on a compliance agreement that gives the
district time--often years--to find needed funds or build capabilities.
Once local officials make a promise, they are highly vulnerable to
charges of nonimplementation. Likewise, a district that promised to
report progress, e.g., in desegregating classrooms, is open to charges
of fraud if it falsifies the reports.[8] Individual local officials
also know that their reputations are at risk if they fail to deliver on
a promise to OCR.

These considerations apply, however, only to those changes that are
unambiguously agreed to. In practice, glittering generalities or
ambiguous promises mean little. General pledges of nondiscrimination or
promises to improve planning or accountability processes can be ignored
with impunity. Most compliance agreements include such statements,
inserted by OCR in an effort to broaden the effects of its actions. OCR
officials believe that such generalities may provide a warrant for more
aggressive enforcement should OCR receive further complaints from the
same district (we know of no instances where this happened). But they
seldom establish effective frameworks for voluntary local compliance
processes.

_____

    [8] Theoretically, OCR could re-open a complaint if follow-up
reports were insufficient or suspect. However, we found few instances
where these reports were ever read, much less used as leverage for
further action.

In our interviews, we tried to learn whether the <u>process</u> by which an LEA responded to OCR determined whether the local school district would make substantive changes in its activities. We asked, "Are districts that perceive enforcement as a crisis especially likely to make changes in educational services?" Based on our fieldwork, the answer to that question is negative. Local school districts reacting to their first brushes with OCR enforcement are no less likely than more experienced districts to make major changes in their instructional programs.

However, LEAs reacting to their first OCR dealings are likely to make more procedural changes and agree to them sooner. Neophyte districts are more likely to take extreme first-negotiation positions-- either of total intransigence or of overeagerness to appease OCR--but most ultimately find a moderate position before their first case is closed. Such LEAs pay very high process costs in their first contacts with OCR. But since many of these costs are self-imposed by the local school district, OCR gains little leverage.

Districts that have established bureaucratic routines pay lower process costs because the stresses of dealing with OCR are delegated to a few specialists. The specialists' skills and experience can also lower OCR's process costs. Most know the law well enough to recognize a <u>prima</u> <u>facie</u> valid complaint, and will initiate corrective action before OCR investigates. Experienced local personnel can get to the heart of an issue and identify the real points for negotiation very quickly. Some get to know OCR staff well enough to build relationships of personal trust. Negotiations and exchange of information are greatly eased thereby. OCR regional office personnel--from investigators to regional directors--all agreed that they would rather deal with local compliance coordinators than inexperienced school administrators.

A few local officials use their expertise to raise OCR's process costs. One local attorney reported that he routinely filed a legal memorandum questioning whether each specific Title IX complaint fits within OCR's mandate. Officials from several districts--all of whom have the same attorney--now refuse to gather any information for OCR. In response to OCR's information requests, they write, "Our files are open. Come and get the data you need." Another district refuses to negotiate any corrective actions until OCR lawyers have defined the district's violation in writing.[9] These tactics make OCR's job much harder. Initial notification of complaints must be written with great care; site visits take longer than usual; bluffing does not pay off; and negotiations are long, formalized, and laborious.

Several of our interview respondents--both local officials and OCR staff--cited instances of local experts forcing OCR to sharpen its investigative plans, focus its requests for information, and improve its statements of legal issues. These tactics force OCR to redo work that might have passed less informed scrutiny. They may also lead OCR to abandon further efforts on behalf of a vague, legally questionable, or very complex complaint.

It is clear from our interviews, however, that OCR is not frightened off by experienced local negotiators. Some regional offices strategically assign their best staff and do their most thorough work in dealing with such LEAs. The majority of complaints against experienced school districts are settled with "violation-corrected" agreements.[10]

In some instances, LEAs' use of attorneys and compliance specialists may improve the outcomes of civil rights enforcement. Local experts who are aware of the school district's legal responsibilities can fix some problems on their own once they know of an OCR investigation. They can force OCR to improve the quality and discipline of its own work; they can negotiate efficiently; and they provide a clear locus of responsibility for the implementation of remedies.

---

[9] Both OCR and local officials believe this strategy is becoming more prevalent under the Reagan Administration's policy of emphasizing negotiation and minimizing federal intervention. Numerous respondents (especially those we interviewed in the summer and fall of 1981) mentioned the mere handful of "violation" letters of findings (LOFs) that had been issued since the Reagan Administration took office.

[10] Of course, a "violation-corrected" finding does not prove that a school district is in full compliance; it could mean that OCR did not seek remedies for all possible violations discovered in the course of a review or investigation (which could be a useful leverage in negotiations). Analysis of these "false negatives" is beyond the scope of this study.

Evidence from OSE Experience

This section has focused on OCR rather than on OSE because of the former's greater reliance on enforcement. OSE does, however, use classic enforcement methods from time to time in dealing with SEAs. OSE has conducted very close reviews of state special education plans and monitored state administrative practices; it also has threatened to impose fiscal sanctions on several SEAs. OSE's limited experience conforms to the general patterns reported above for OCR. Most SEAs treated the first OSE enforcement actions as crises: Their response processes were highly disorganized and regular work was disrupted. After their first experiences, states developed more routine, low-cost ways of dealing with OSE. OSE has succeeded in negotiating important changes in state plans and procedures, and states have honored their commitments. OSE's enforcement efforts, like OCR's, have been most successful in changing administrative procedures rather than educational services.

Beneficiary Responses to Enforcement

During our fieldwork it became evident that few of the people who initiated complaints were satisfied with the outcome. Many thought that the enforcement process had failed them. Disappointed complainants frequently questioned OCR's commitment and competence. Many complainants were distressed that they were never contacted by the OCR staff who conducted a site visit to investigate their complaints.

The enforcement process inevitably creates dissatisfaction. OCR investigators must maintain a degree of professional detachment from complainants' problems, and also build productive working relationships with local officials. Some complainants regard nonconfrontational tactics by OCR as evidence of collusion. In addition, many complainants we spoke with were unfamiliar with the extent of OCR's authority and expected help that OCR simply could not give them. It is not surprising that they were displeased with the results of an investigation that produced a written policy of nondiscrimination when they were hoping for, say, a monetary award. Moreover, it is likely that some complainants hope that OCR will intervene on their behalf in complex

local disputes that they can only define subjectively. No outcome
within OCR's power is likely to satisfy those complainants.[11]

PROMOTION

Effects on Decisionmaking Processes

Promotion is a subtler strategy than enforcement and its effects
are far harder to trace. OSE's promotional activities are all founded
in PL 94-142; even if OSE were replaced with a simple check-writing
bureau, PL 94-142 would create local pressures for improvements in
special education. In many communities, parents of handicapped children
were an effective interest group for several years before PL 94-142 was
enacted. Even in the absence of a federal statute, those groups would
have obtained some new benefits for handicapped children. The effects
of the statute, OSE's efforts, and local interest group activities are
hopelessly confounded.[12] Recognizing the impossibility of quantifying
the unique contribution of OSE's promotional efforts, the best we can do
is to identify those local activities in which OSE's activity has been a
necessary ingredient.

---

[11] In one OCR region we visited, one man had submitted 25
complaints in the past year. His complaints--each against a different
school district--typically raised more than 40 separate issues. OCR
staff assigned to the cases reported that the complaints often misstated
the applicable law and the existing local circumstances. In the opinion
of OCR investigators, the complainant hoped that OCR would intervene on
his behalf to settle a variety of old political scores. Because the
complainant would not amend his allegations or meet with the local
school districts and OCR to negotiate settlements, the complaints
created little, if any, pressure for change. OCR was forced to spend
thousands of person-hours interpreting and trying to investigate the
complaints, and the respondent school districts had to spend time and
money responding to OCR. OCR was thrust into the position of imposing
process costs on the school districts to no purpose. Many school
districts complained to Congress about the process costs, thus creating
a difficult political environment for top OCR Washington and regional
officials. Meanwhile, the complainant won nothing and sought local
newspaper publicity for his view that OCR was unwilling to fight for the
victims of discrimination.
[12] The text understates the complexity of relationships among
OSE, PL 94-142, and local interest groups. OSE is not simply a creation
of the statute; its bureaucratic predecessors helped engineer the
legislative coalition that enacted PL 94-142. Likewise, local interest
groups did not all predate PL 94-142; most, in fact, were organized
after the statute was enacted and many were established with direct help
from OSE.

The most important of these events are the creation of
individualized education plans and the resolution of disputes through
due process hearings. These two activities are required by PL 94-142,
but their quality is due largely to OSE's efforts. As was explained
above, OSE's enforcement led SEAs to implement the IEP and due process
provisions much more carefully than they would have on their own. OSE
training, technical assistance, and advocacy alerted special education
professionals to the leverage that the IEP and due process requirements
created for them. Parents trained in OSE-sponsored workshops counseled
other parents on potential uses of the IEP. OSE pamphlets and training
materials were sent to many parents of handicapped children. Well-
organized local parent groups volunteered to help parents in other
LEAs to get organized. OSE disseminated the results of important due
process hearings so that parents everywhere could know what services
they could demand for their children. Local administrators used the
fact of growing parent assertiveness to get increased special education
appropriations.

As several of the local officials we interviewed said, special
education advocacy organizations--professionals and parents--are the
most influential interest groups involved in local school affairs. Even
in districts where they were well organized before the enactment of PL
94-142, their influence has grown enormously in the past seven years.
OSE's information campaigns and training were essential factors in that
growth of influence. PL 94-142 established a framework that special
education advocates could use to advance their interests. OSE's
promotion efforts showed the advocates how to use the framework, and
urged them to do so assiduously.

Districts' reactions to their first IEP and due process cases were
disorganized--very similar to the reactions to enforcement described
above. By 1981, however, every LEA in the country (with the exception
of districts in New Mexico) had processed multiple IEPs, and most had
handled at least one due process hearing. The districts had long since
passed through their crisis periods and established clear routines and
lines of administrative authority (usually in the form of well-staffed
special education divisions in the central office for handling parent-

initiated demands and disputes).[13] These routines, however, did not reduce parents' leverage. Local special education offices manage very active local bargaining processes. Parents bargain with special education providers about the services their children receive. Providers inform parents about promising new treatments for specific handicaps, and thus encourage new demands for services. When the educators cannot provide the services that parents demand, parents and professionals combine to demand increases in special education funding. Local school boards and superintendents use the fact of growing parent demand as a rationale for increased state special education funding.

Nearly all demands and grievances are negotiated at the local level. Our respondents estimated that fewer than 25 percent of parents contest the professionals' judgment or make specific requests in the preparation of their children's IEPs. Apparently (based on very limited data), fewer than 1 percent of the handicapped children in the public schools are ever involved in due process hearings.[14] However, as our respondents consistently said, the availability of the IEP and fair hearing procedures makes school personnel more responsive to the desires of parents of handicapped children than to those of any other group. Most bargaining takes place on the threshold of the official IEP process between parents and professionals, all of whom would prefer to avoid the cost and inconvenience of formal procedures.

Effects on Substantive Policy and Practice

The analytical difficulties that dogged the previous section are even greater here. One cannot validly attribute all of the recent changes in special education practices to OSE's activity; but promotion was definitely a key contribution to those changes.

----

[13] For an extensive discussion of how school districts respond to due process hearings and litigation, see Paul T. Hill, Educational Policymaking Through the Civil Justice System, The Rand Corporation, R-2904-ICJ (forthcoming).

[14] Quantitative data about the use of the IEP and due process are very difficult to obtain. Few states or localities keep records about how many parents make specific demands in the preparation of their children's IEPs, and data about the incidence of due process hearings are very scanty.

Changes that our local respondents attributed to OSE's promotional activity include:

o   Quick adoption of new special education practices. OSE's technical assistance programs ensure that local special education staff and parents learn quickly about new therapies and instructional techniques. Parents and educators can use the leverage available through the IEP and fair hearing processes to get such services delivered.

o   Implementation of new legal doctrines. OSE disseminates, both directly and through its grantees, the results of landmark court cases (e.g., on autistic children's rights to year-round schooling). Local special educators use this information to press for changes in general district policies, and parents formulate corresponding demands in negotiations over children's IEPs.

o   Extension of services to the vast majority of handicapped children. OSE's emphasis on "child find" through technical assistance, publicity, and assistance to parent organizations has greatly increased the numbers of handicapped children receiving special education.

o   General increases in the quality and professionalism of special education staff. OSE's support for schools of education and in-service teacher training, coupled with the growth in funding for special education, has greatly increased the number and apparent qualifications of local special education teachers.

o   Increases in special education's share of the total education budget. Local interest groups, encouraged by OSE and buttressed by PL 94-142's guarantee of free appropriate public education for all handicapped children, have effectively lobbied school boards and state legislatures for budget increases. Until 1979, special education was the fastest growing element of state and local education budgets. More recently, as real education expenditures in states' and local school districts' budgets have been stagnant or declining, special education has lost less purchasing power than any other class of services.

The true picture is not all rosy. As we saw in some LEAs, some of the service gains made through the fair hearing process are more apparent than real. When special education budgets are fixed, expensive services awarded to a few students reduce the pool of resources available for services to others. According to the best existing data on due process hearings,[15] nearly half the cases concern parents' requests for expensive private educational placements. Awards to parents in such cases cost, on average, more than twice as much per student as special education delivered by LEAs. Special education directors in several districts told us that those awards forced reductions in other services, e.g., fewer resources for evaluation of students, longer waiting times for students awaiting placement, and fractionally larger class sizes.[16]

There are clearly limits to the potential substantive gains to be had from a promotional strategy. Special education ultimately competes with other classes of educational services, and with public services in general, for funds. Promotion can improve special education's relative position, but it cannot always produce real gains for its intended beneficiaries. As we have seen, however, promotion is a very effective strategy in the proper circumstances.

Section V will identify the appropriate circumstances for promotion and enforcement, as well as for other possible federal influence strategies. It will provide, as far as our data permit, an assessment of the limits, costs, and best uses of the different federal influence strategies.

---

[15] Kirst and Bertken, op. cit.
[16] For a broader discussion of the phenomenon of cross-subsidy among student beneficiaries of federal education programs, see Jackie Kimbrough and Paul Hill, The Aggregate Effects of Federal Education Programs, The Rand Corporation, R-2638-ED, September 1981.

V. CHOOSING FEDERAL INFLUENCE STRATEGIES

To this point, the report has focused on the first objective
established in Sec. I: to identify the Department of Education's
strategies for influencing school districts and explain how these
strategies work. This section addresses the report's second objective:
to apply what we have learned to broader questions about the capacities
and limits of federal efforts to influence state and local policy, and
about the likely costs and benefits of such efforts. Our analysis is
based on our data on the Office for Civil Rights and the Office of
Special Education. We believe, however, that it may apply more broadly
to any federal effort to influence state and local policy,[1] as shown
in the following discussion, where we relate our propositions to
education and other fields.

Our purpose is to help federal policymakers--both the members of
Congress who establish new goals and allocate resources to programs, and
the officials of the Executive Branch who decide how and when program
resources will be used--to understand the tools available to them. The
analysis should also be useful to interest group leaders, state and
local officials, and students of intergovernmental relations, all of
whom are trying to understand and influence the federal government's
regulatory posture.

This section presents a framework that identifies the factors that
the federal government should consider in deciding whether and how to
try to change state and local government activities. The intent of the
framework is to identify governmental influence strategies most likely
to effect change in the face of certain preexisting conditions at the
state and local level. As such, it is intended for program design
considerations. We also discuss the kinds of costs that the federal
government must be prepared to bear if it hopes to influence other

---

[1] Evidence from other sources suggests that problems of
intergovernmental relations are similar from one field to another. See
Bardach and Kagan, op. cit.; Stone, op. cit.; and the case studies in
James Q. Wilson (ed.), The Politics of Regulation, Basic Books, New
York, 1980.

levels of government. Finally, we discuss practical factors that limit and complicate the application of our generalizations.

THE FRAMEWORK

Our framework has two major elements: Given federal program goals, there may be barriers to the attainment of those goals, and specific strategies may overcome those barriers. The framework is meant to apply to any federal program goal that requires state or local governments to change their policies and services. It definitely encompasses the goals of OSE's and OCR's programs, and appears to apply to programs in such diverse domestic policy areas as housing, criminal justice, environmental protection, and economic development. (Data and the relevant literature for these other policy areas being sparse, however, we suggest that our framework be used as propositions for future research.)

The existence of a federal program goal implies some acknowledged need to change state or local activities. The essential common purpose of federal domestic programs is to help or induce states, localities, and firms to do things that they would not do if left on their own. Federal policies and programs are therefore meant to overcome any barriers to achieving the desired outcomes. The possible barriers fit into five categories:

o   Technical intractability--the absence of the materials, machinery, or skills required to attain a goal;

o   Lack of support--unwillingness on the part of state or local officeholders, service providers, or citizens to make the necessary changes;

o   Opposition--resistance to the necessary changes from state or local officeholders, service providers, or citizens;

o   Lack of knowledge--inability of local service providers to implement the necessary changes; and

o   Lack of resources--the absence of funds required to pay for the necessary changes.

Federal program strategies--ways of overcoming these barriers--
also fit into five broad categories:

o   Research and development, which provides the basic information
    and techniques necessary to attain program goals; and

o   Enforcement, which relies on federal monitoring and sanctioning
    of local compliance with rules that require actions in support
    of program goals;

o   Technical assistance, which disseminates skills to service
    providers; [2]

o   Promotion, which helps local beneficiaries to organize in
    support of program goals;

o   Subsidy, which provides the funds required to offset the costs
    of changes in state or local activities.

The strategies form an incentive structure--that is, they provide
reasons for people and governments to change behaviors and policies.
Each strategy is linked to one of the barriers. For example, research
and development addresses problems of technical intractability; the
other obvious matches are enforcement with opposition, promotion with
support, technical assistance with lack of knowledge, and subsidy with
lack of resources. Some of the strategies have side-effects that affect
barriers other than the ones to which they are logically connected. The
following subsections show how the strategies work to overcome
particular barriers.

Federal Program Goals

Our framework assumes the existence of a federal program goal,
specified by the Congress, the Executive Branch, or the courts.
Establishment of a goal means that at least one branch of government
supports it. National gun control is an example of a potential goal
that has not achieved official endorsement; protection of air and water
quality is an example of a goal that has been officially endorsed.

_____
    [2] In our analysis of OSE we found that technical assistance was
so integrated with promotion that the two could not be separated. The

The mechanisms and processes by which goals are authoritatively established are outside the scope of our current interest.[3] The complex processes required to establish goals ensure that they are rarely arbitrary or random. Some goals, however, may have to be ultimately abandoned or reformulated because they exceed the government's influence capacity; one example is Prohibition. Other goals may be abandoned because the obstacles they face are insurmountable, such as the World War II effort to encourage people to eat organ meats. Still other goals may be in effect abandoned or reformulated because the activities to be changed are too numerous, subtle, or widely dispersed to be supervised; laws regulating sexual relationships between consenting adults exemplify this.

Barriers to Overcome

Tractability. Goals vary in technical feasibility. Some goals (e.g., the building of the interstate highway system) require only the application of existing machinery, materials, and skills. Other possible goals, such as the elimination of all air pollutants from industrial sources, are technically feasible but only at astronomical cost (e.g., the abandonment of all pollution-causing industrial activities). Some possible goals--for example, eliminating cancer-- are not now feasible at any cost.

Federal efforts to influence state and local policy are appropriate only if the goal is tractable. Intergovernmental incentives (whether created through enforcement, promotion, or subsidy) cannot overcome the lack of technical capacity. Government programs that ignore the issue of tractability are likely to backfire, ultimately discrediting the program and the government itself. The Environmental Protection

---

logical distinction is clear, however, and we shall therefore separate technical assistance and promotion for purposes of this section.

[3] Some case studies that discuss these mechanisms and processes are: Eric Redman, The Dance of Legislation, Simon and Schuster, New York, 1973; T. R. Reid, Congressional Odyssey, W. H. Freeman, San Francisco, 1980; Donald L. Horowitz, The Courts and Social Policy, The Brookings Institution, Washington, D.C., 1977; and Daniel A. Mazmanion and Jeanne Nienaber, Can Organizations Change? The Brookings Institution, Washington, D.C., 1979.

Agency's standards for municipal waste water treatment are a good
example: Many communities installed the best available technologies but
were still unable to meet the water quality standards. As a result, the
government's whole structure of water quality regulation is now under
political attack. Federal standards for auto exhaust emissions provide
a slightly different example. Though the standards were feasible under
existing technologies, costs were prohibitive. Automakers' concern for
the competitiveness of the U.S. auto industry forced EPA to postpone and
significantly relax its standards. In both examples, the federal
government suffered two kinds of losses as a result of its failure to
consider tractability: First, standards were reduced dramatically to
levels lower than available technologies could support; and second, the
federal agency and its broad mission of environmental protection were
subjected to political attack.

Tractability, then, is important for federal strategy. If the goal
is not tractable, the federal government's problem is either to overcome
technical barriers through research and development, or to reformulate
the goal in light of real capabilities. If the goal is tractable, the
federal government can select strategies that create support at the
local level and ensure that local actors have the necessary competence
and funding.

Support and Opposition. Support refers to local actors'
willingness to implement a change; opposition refers to antagonism
toward a change. Some federal goals have strong local support, while
others are controversial, broadly unpopular, or seen as unimportant.
Some goals (such as creating public service jobs in areas of high
unemployment), may be very popular, but most goals meet at least some
local opposition. The federal goals of urban renewal and interstate
highway construction generally got support from community leaders, but
drew opposition from people whose residences and places of business were
displaced or disrupted. Federal efforts to create public service jobs
got support from local governments and unemployed workers (although some
were concerned about what would happen when the funds ceased), but were
occasionally opposed by businesses that depend on a good supply of low-
wage workers.

The level of local support has definite implications for federal strategy. If local support for a goal is strong, the federal government needs only to ensure that supporters have the necessary resources (including access to decisionmaking processes) and technical skills. If local opposition is overwhelming, the federal government needs to recognize that progress toward the goal may be arduous and slow; it is also likely that the federal government will have to exert continuous pressure on local officials. If local opposition is strong, the federal government needs to impose countervailing legal or political pressure. That is the specific purpose of enforcement--to raise the costs so noncompliance is prohibitive. If local opinion is indifferent--i.e., if support and opposition are both weak--the federal government needs to encourage existing supporters and create new ones. Enforcement can help overcome the lack of support, but as OSE's success demonstrates, promotion can be very effective in strengthening existing bases of support for federal program goals.

Knowledge. Knowledge refers to local ability to operate the programs necessary to attain the goal. Knowledge and tractability are different. A goal is tractable if the requisite expertise, equipment, organization, etc., exist somewhere. But a tractable goal cannot be attained if local governments or firms lack the requisite skills. Soil conservation, for example, was a tractable goal, but it could not be attained until the U.S. Department of Agriculture trained farmers in new methods of land management. Similarly, the goal of immunizing all children against polio could not be achieved until the federal government provided technical training and the vaccine to local public health officials. In education, many school systems lack the trained personnel necessary to deliver bilingual education, especially in the languages of new Asian immigrants.[4]

Again, the level of local knowledge should affect the federal government's strategy. If local actors have all the knowledge necessary to achieve a goal, the federal government needs only to overcome obstacles, if any, created by lack of funds or local support. If local

_____

[4] Patricia C. Gandara, The Implementation of Language Assistance Programs, The Rand Corporation (forthcoming).

actors lack the requisite knowledge, the federal government must provide it by training, technical assistance, or loans of personnel.

Resources. Resources here are the funds to pay for desired changes in state or local activities. Changes in services delivered, equipment installed, or management systems used nearly always cost money. Even if new activities supplant old ones, most changes involve some increases in net expenditures. Since the mid-1970s, most states and localities have experienced fixed or declining revenues; new activities, therefore, require either compensating cuts in existing services or financial assistance from outside. Cuts in existing state or local services are very difficult for anyone to engineer, and sometimes impossible for the federal government to mandate. Thus, in many cases, the activities required by a federal program goal must be supported by a subsidy.

Behind this simple principle--that new federally desired activities usually require subsidies--is a set of very complex problems. It is very difficult to estimate a priori what the gross costs of new services will be; what the net costs will be, given the prior level of local expenditure on similar services; what the real-cost differences among states and localities will be; and what the minimum amount of subsidy is that will induce states and localities to comply.

The last issue is particularly thorny, because it confounds objective considerations of costs with subjective considerations of local support for the program goal. If the dominant local interests have no sympathy for the program goal, they might permit the desired changes only if subsidies equal or exceed costs. The basic subsidy lets the local agency change its activities at no cost; the extra subsidy provides unrestricted funds that the local agency can use for its own purposes. If, on the other hand, the dominant local interests favor the change, partial subsidies may be sufficient. A partial subsidy (e.g., a matching grant) biases local decisionmaking in favor of a federal program goal by greatly reducing the unit price of the desired activities.[5]

_____

[5] In times of scarce resources, states and localities are apt to view the promise of matching funds with skepticism. They are fearful of "buying into" noncritical programs that deflect funds (however small) from priority areas. They are also concerned about creating programs and clientele groups that will be difficult to appease if federal

Examples of all three kinds of subsidy are easy to find. Programs that pay the full and exact costs of services delivered include compensatory education for disadvantaged students and Medicaid. The former pays all costs in advance and the latter reimburses for costs once they are incurred, but both pay (or at least were designed to pay) exact full costs. Though it is hard to find existing programs that pay more than full costs, there is at least one partial example, the Emergency School Aid Act, which paid the direct costs of desegregating schools plus the costs of additional services proposed by the LEA.[6] Matching programs include Aid to Families with Dependent Children, Vocational Education, interstate highway construction, and sewage treatment grants.

In general, goals that entail costly new state or local activities require some federal subsidy. The type and amount of subsidy required depend on two factors: first, the cost of the required changes, and second, the degree to which local officials and interest groups want to make changes. Whether a goal requires a partial subsidy, a full subsidy, or a greater-than-full subsidy depends on the level of local support for the goal being sought. Since, as we have seen above, lack of support can also be addressed in part by enforcement and promotion, the choice of a subsidy type should be made in conjunction with choices about whether and how to use promotion and enforcement.

---

support ceases, leaving them to pick up the additional costs. For a general review of the effects of federal grants on local governmental expenditures, see Edward M. Gramlich, "Intergovernmental Grants: A Review of the Empirical Literature," in Wallace Oates (ed.), The Political Economy of Fiscal Federalism, Lexington Books, Lexington, Massachusetts, 1977, pp. 219-239.

[6] Some programs intended to pay exact full costs may in fact pay greater than full costs. Many localities reduce their own spending in areas that become supported by federal grants. Econometric estimates of the total increase in local expenditures caused by each dollar of federal grants range from zero to over seventy cents. ESEA Title I, the best known performer in this respect, creates increases in total local expenditures at a rate of less than 75 cents on the dollar. Conclusions about Title I are based on analysis conducted by Martin Feldstein and reported in National Institute of Education, Title I Funds Allocation: The Current Formula, 1977, pp. 83-89.

USING THE FRAMEWORK TO CHOOSE STRATEGIES

Figure 1 shows how our framework can be used to select strategies. The figure identifies circumstances under which the five strategies (research and development, technical assistance, subsidy, enforcement, and promotion) should be used, both singly and in combinations. Logically, except for tractability, the barriers have no rank-order of importance; their presence or absence should be assessed simultaneously, not sequentially. Like all such schemes, this one oversimplifies reality. It assumes, in particular, that it is possible to generalize about the levels of support, local knowledge, and finances that attach to a particular goal.

As Fig. 1 indicates, some circumstances require a single influence strategy, and others require several. The combination of barriers and resultant strategies is displayed in Table 4, which follows each of the possible paths through the framework. For example, an enforcement strategy is called for if the only barrier to be overcome is local opposition: If the goal is tractable and local knowledge and resources are sufficient, there is no need for R&D, promotion, technical assistance, or subsidy, since enforcement directly compensates for the lack of local support. Similarly, a subsidy strategy is called for if the only barrier to be overcome is lack of funds. If local actors are willing and technically able to act, enforcement and promotion are unnecessary. Only subsidy is needed to pay the real costs of changing local services.

Multiple strategies are necessary to overcome multiple barriers. For example, goals that lack support and exceed local technical knowledge require both promotion and technical assistance. Since many goals require resources (and since providing funds can be a potent way of overcoming opposition or indifference), subsidy is a necessary component of many federal programs. However, goals that require only subsidy are probably rare. Most federal goals--including the ones pursued by OCR and OSE--require efforts to increase local support, overcome local opposition, or increase local technical capacity, in addition to subsidy. Most goals also require either enforcement to overcome local opposition, or promotion to strengthen local support and technical capacity.

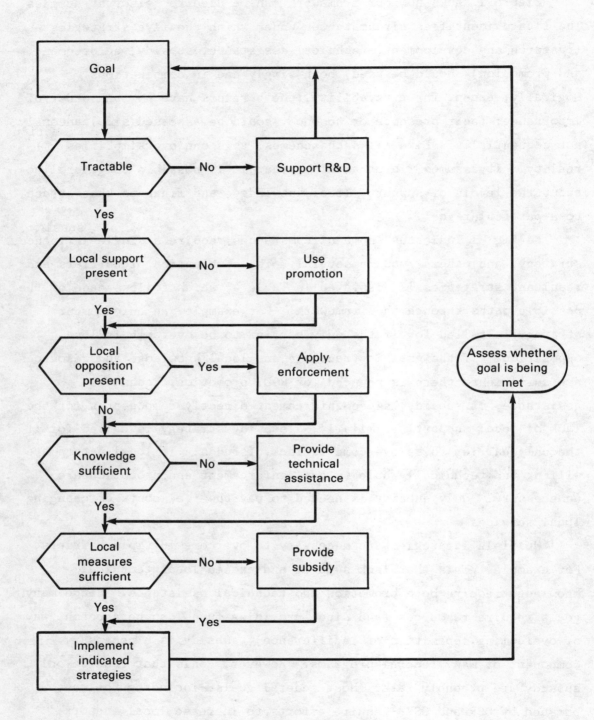

Fig. 1 -- Using the framework to choose strategies

Table 4

COMBINATIONS OF BARRIERS AND RESULTANT STRATEGIES

Tractability	Support	Opposition	Knowledge	Resources	Strategy
−					R&D
+	−	−	−	−	Promotion, TA,[a] subsidy
+	+	−	−	−	TA, subsidy
+	+	+	−	−	Enforcement, TA, subsidy
+	+	+	+	−	Enforcement, subsidy
+	+	+	+	+	Enforcement
+	−	+	+	+	Promotion, enforcement
+	−	−	+	+	Promotion
+	−	−	−	+	Promotion, TA
+	+	−	+	+	Self-fulfilling
+	+	−	−	+	TA
+	+	+	−	+	Enforcement, TA
+	+	−	+	−	Subsidy
+	−	+	−	−	Promotion, enforcement, TA, subsidy
+	−	+	+	−	Promotion, enforcement, subsidy
+	−	−	+	−	Promotion, subsidy
+	−	+	−	+	Promotion, enforcement, TA

[a]Technical assistance.

NOTE: + = presence of; − = absence of.

Though the framework has already become complex, it needs to be more elaborate still. It ignores three important factors that inevitably affect the choice of influence strategies: disagreement over goals, variability of local conditions, and the implication of the kind and level of costs that must be paid.

DISAGREEMENT OVER GOALS

Federal goals may not always be as clear as our framework assumes. Compromises in the legislative process can produce laws whose real purposes are equivocal. ESEA Title I is an excellent example: The Act's legislative history shows that some supporters saw it as a source of unconstrained general aid to school districts, while others saw it as a source of tightly constrained grants solely for the education of low-income children. Supporters of the latter view won out, but only after many years of bureaucratic infighting and statutory amendment.

When the goal of a program is in dispute, conflict and confusion about influence strategies are inevitable. Since all factions hope to benefit from the program, they are reluctant to call attention to their differences over goals. They focus their energies on trying to get the federal government to use the influence strategies that are most compatible with their goals. Conflict over goals is often resolved in compromises over influence strategies.

Examples of fighting over strategies as proxies for goals abound. The histories of several major education programs, including ESEA Title I, PL 94-142, and vocational education have been marked by disputes over whether the federal government should use enforcement, promotion, or subsidy as its principal influence strategy. Those disputes masked broader disagreements about program goals--specifically, about whether federal funds were to be used at local officials' discretion or for a limited set of federally specified purposes. People who wanted to achieve the former felt that local support would be easy to obtain and, therefore, favored a promotional strategy. Those who wanted to target funds toward low-income groups felt that net local support was weak, and therefore favored an enforcement strategy.

When program goals are in dispute, our framework cannot identify the one best influence strategy for the federal government to use. It can, however, help the contending factions identify the best strategies for achieving their particular goals. At this writing, for example, there is real uncertainty about the goals and appropriate influence strategies for a major federal education program. Chapter 1 of the 1981 Education Consolidation and Improvement Act authorizes a program of federal aid to school districts serving large numbers of low-income children. The program is obviously meant to be a successor to ESEA Title I, but the legislation is artfully vague about both goals and influence strategies.[6] Some supporters claim that the program is meant, like Title I, to provide compensatory services targeted directly on low-achieving children in poverty schools. Others claim that the program is meant to provide funds for the general upgrading of schools in low-income areas. The latter group assume that their version of the program's goal is perfectly compatible with the preferences of local school boards and that local educators know best how to use the funds. According to our framework, that group will prefer subsidy as their only influence strategy. People in the former group, however, assume that local school boards will not automatically target program funds on low-achieving, poor students, and do not think local educators know how to serve such students effectively. According to our framework, that group will prefer an influence strategy that includes enforcement and promotion, as well as subsidy. Political infighting about that program's future has just begun, but the predicted patterns of conflict over influence methods are already apparent.

VARIABILITY OF LOCAL CONDITIONS

Variations in local conditions make it very difficult for policymakers to assess the presence or absence of barriers. Every state

_____

[7] For an analysis of this new direction and states' initial responses, see Linda Darling-Hammond and Ellen L. Marks, The New Federalism in Education: State Responses to the 1981 Education Consolidation and Improvement Act, The Rand Corporation, R-3008-ED (forthcoming).

and locality is likely to have its own structure of support and
opposition, mix of skills, and available resources. An ideal federal
strategy would acknowledge and build upon the incentive structures,
skills, and dollars available in each community. More realistically,
federal influence strategies should at least be tailored to fit the
circumstances that exist in as many communities as possible.

Efforts on behalf of such diverse goals as school desegregation,
reduction of air pollution, and reduction of highway traffic speed, have
all encountered wide variations in local support. Knowledge is also
unevenly distributed. Some local governments lack the skill or
equipment to detect violations of air pollution standards, to identify
sound investments in urban redevelopment, or to deliver sophisticated
forms of bilingual instruction. Such localities present very different
problems for federal influence efforts than do governments that have the
necessary equipment and trained personnel.

The framework identifies the strategies that are logically best
suited for particular circumstances, but it does not consider the costs
of using the alternative strategies. In designing a program, the
rational policymaker will ask not only whether a particular strategy
fits the circumstances, but also whether it is the least costly.

THE COSTS OF FEDERAL INFLUENCE

All of the influence strategies in our framework impose costs on
the federal government.

The costs of support for research and development are financial.
They may take the form of contracts or grant awards, establishment of
special organizations (e.g., the National Institutes of Health), or tax
incentives for the private sector.

The costs of subsidy are also financial. It involves direct
transfers of federal funds to state or local governments to pay for
desired changes. To receive a subsidy, the state or locality needs to
guarantee that it will use grant funds to make the changes (in its
services, organizational procedures, or whatever) that the federal
government intends. In theory, subsidies let local governments provide

new services thought desirable by the federal government at no cost to themselves.

The costs of promotion are measured in federal funds for developing professions dedicated to program purposes, and for helping local groups organize and gain access to local decision processes. These costs are high, but usually less than the costs of subsidy.

The costs of technical assistance most often appear as in-kind contributions, used to improve local expertise for service delivery. Technical assistance may include training workshops, information dissemination, or expert advice.

The costs of enforcement are largely political. Political costs arise whenever a government action hurts or offends a politically powerful person or interest group. Any government action that establishes a new rule reduces someone's freedom and creates displeasure. Cost-shifting creates opposition (e.g., requiring states or localities to pay for something desired by the federal government). In general, the political costs of a governmental action are a function of the opposition that action stimulates. By letting itself become the target of any opposition generated by a change in local policy, the federal government assumes the political costs of the change by taking (or appearing to take) decisions out of the hands of local officials.

When establishing a new program, the government can make some choices about the kinds of costs it wants to pay. Other things being equal, the federal government pays smaller political costs for a program that emphasizes cash subsidies; conversely, the government can accept political costs in lieu of providing subsidies by strongly enforcing a requirement.

Attempts to use a single influence strategy may impose enormous political, in-kind, or financial costs on the government--costs so high that decisionmakers may be unwilling to accept them. Policymakers may, therefore, try complex combinations of influence strategies, hoping to pay more moderate levels of subsidy, promotional assistance, and political costs. For example, a full federal subsidy for PL 94-142 would have cost nearly $10 billion instead of the $1 billion that was actually provided. OSE's promotional effort--an in-kind assistance effort costing less than $150 million per year--helped advocacy groups and practitioners exert enormous leverage on state and local budgets. OSE's small enforcement effort enhanced the effectiveness of its subsidies and promotion at a relatively low level of political cost. Even the most aggressive "enforcement" efforts have been alloyed with some features of subsidy and promotion. For example, early school desegregation efforts assumed political costs (openly coercing governors by stationing federal troops around schools and colleges) and provided few subsidies or in-kind donations. Later, with the enactment of the Emergency School Aid Act, the federal government began paying some financial as well as political costs.

But there are, however, strict limits to the substitution of one influence strategy (and thus one form of cost) for another. Enforcement, no matter how aggressive and politically costly it is, cannot work if a goal is technically intractable or if local officials lack the skills to make necessary changes in services. Subsidy, no matter how great, cannot overcome lack of knowledge. Likewise, promotion, no matter how comprehensive and skillfully done, cannot overcome total local opposition or lack of funds.

Use of the wrong influence method can impose enormous costs to no effect. The failure of the Department of Education's 1979 draft bilingual education regulations illustrates the point. The regulations were designed as unfunded mandates: They would have required local school districts to raid their own budgets in order to pay for an ambitious program of identifying, testing, serving, and evaluating language minority students. Educators and school board members in many districts did not want to spend as much on bilingual education as the proposed rules would have required; nor did they think the prescribed approach was the technically best available. Opposition to the requirements forced the Secretary to withdraw them in early 1981. In that case, the federal government's effort to avoid paying any financial costs created political costs greater than either the Carter or Reagan Administration was willing to pay, and the whole effort had to be abandoned.

Because goals are often in dispute, circumstances differ from one place to another, and policymakers will not support programs that are prohibitively costly, most federal programs rely on mixed influence strategies. Most federal programs use hybrid approaches that combine elements of subsidy, promotion, technical assistance, and enforcement.

The Importance of Hybrid Approaches

The preceding discussion has presented a few hybrid approaches, and many more can be found. To halt the spread of venereal diseases, the federal government sponsors public awareness campaigns (promotion) and health clinics (subsidy). The 55-mph speed limit was implemented by educating people about safety and gasoline consumption advantages (promotion), and then backed by penalties for offenders (enforcement). The government follows a rather convoluted approach in the tobacco arena: Farmers receive cash outlays for their crops (subsidy), the Surgeon General and other public health officials warn of the dangers of cigarette smoking (promotion), and minors are prohibited from purchasing cigarettes (enforcement).

Some of the difficulties encountered by recent federal domestic programs can be attributed to the failure to use the proper combination of influence strategies. OCR's enforcement of Title IX is one example. The statutory prohibition against sex discrimination had a tractable goal, a large group of potential supporters in all localities, some support, and some real uncertainty at the local level about how to implement necessary changes. This suggests a mixed strategy emphasizing technical assistance and promotion, with subsidies and enforcement available if local service changes prove costly or if resistance is encountered. The statute assigned the program to the Office for Civil Rights, which chose only an enforcement strategy. There are several reasons for this apparently mistaken choice: (1) Congress did not want to commit federal subsidy funds; (2) OCR's organizational history predisposes it toward enforcement; and (3) women's groups felt it was necessary for the federal government to assume a confrontational posture, and would have considered subsidies to be unjustified "bribes" to local officials. The unintended consequences are most evident for

OCR, which has been philosophically and legally challenged over its Title IX policies, and the challenge in turn has eroded OCR's credibility in other areas.

The Environmental Protection Agency chose a mixture of enforcement and subsidy to improve local waste-water treatment. EPA was reluctant to train local plant operators or provide technical guidance for plant design, fearing that it would be held accountable for technical failures or legally insufficient advice. Since many localities lacked the requisite technical skills, many of the facilities built with EPA's funds do not clean water to the standards set by law. A technical assistance component to EPA's influence strategy might have lowered the costs of both its enforcement and subsidy efforts, and produced cleaner water.

CONCLUSION

We have tried to present the factors that should determine federal influence strategies broadly enough so that they apply to most policy areas, yet explicitly enough to be applied to individual cases. We count ourselves successful if we have established the following points:

First, the effectiveness of federal influence efforts depends on establishing the correct match between federal program goals and local conditions. For each federal program goal there is a particular combination of local support, knowledge, and available resources; a strategy adapted to that combination will be the most effective.

Second, and conversely, the failure to establish the correct match between federal goals and local conditions creates ineffective, needlessly costly, dysfunctional programs. Poorly selected strategies can inflict large financial and political costs and destroy the federal government's reputation for competence. Haphazard selection of strategies (e.g., large subsidies for all goals when federal funds are plentiful, enforcement of unfunded mandates when money is tight) is a recipe for disaster.

Third, local circumstances also determine the kinds and amounts of costs that the federal government must pay to attain any goal. The federal government must pay different kinds of costs to overcome lack of local support, knowledge, or fiscal resources. The level of any one cost depends on the degree to which local conditions must be changed. Though it is possible to shift some costs from one form to another, the least-cost strategy is usually the one that most directly addresses the local circumstances.

Fourth, no one influence strategy is always the best for all goals or circumstances. The best strategy may differ from time to time and from place to place, and many goals may require complex hybrid strategies. The fact that a strategy worked well for one goal or in one class of jurisdiction does not mean that it will work well for others.

These points are abstract, and the key concepts may be difficult to operationalize in particular circumstances; but as we have shown by our analysis of existing programs, they are at least roughly measurable. If such measurements were made and considered in the design phases of new programs, federal officials could have a far better appreciation of the likely costs and consequences of their strategic choices.

Appendix

ORGANIZATIONAL STRUCTURES OF THE OFFICE FOR CIVIL RIGHTS
AND THE OFFICE OF SPECIAL EDUCATION

OFFICE FOR CIVIL RIGHTS

OCR's organization chart is presented in Fig. 2. There are three
major divisions in OCR headquarters.

The Office of Planning and Compliance Operations (OPCO) is the
least involved of all the offices of OCR in administrative sanctions or
incentives. It has a three-fold mission: (1) to monitor the production
line and paperwork of complaints and compliance reviews, including
setting goals for the regions and ensuring adherence to court-ordered
time lines; (2) to report and monitor what OCR does, which may include
targeting for compliance reviews; and (3) to oversee internal management
of the agency.

The Office of Program Review and Assistance (OPRA) has two
divisions, one for intradepartmental technical assistance and the other
for external technical assistance. The former assists in the process of
diffusing civil rights into departmental-wide concerns. The latter has
two functions: (1) to oversee the regional technical assistance staff;

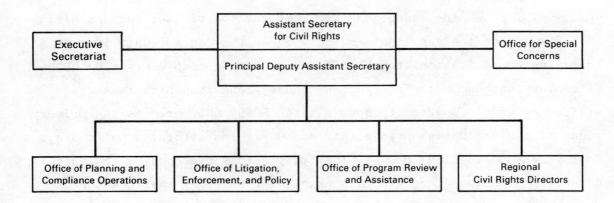

Fig. 2 -- Office for Civil Rights

and (2) to award and administer a series of contracts for technical
assistance (totaling $5 million in FY81). In the past these funds have
typically been used for workshops and information dissemination on
Section 504 (prohibiting discrimination on the basis of handicap)
sponsored by national associations, such as the American Council on
Education, the National Governors Association, and the National League
of Cities.

The Office of Litigation, Enforcement, and Policy is the standard-
setting element of OCR. It is organized into three divisions:
litigation; elementary and secondary education; and postsecondary
education.[1] The Litigation Division is staffed with attorneys who
deal with complaints that have been investigated by the regional
offices, and who are responsible for moving cases to enforcement. They
may call cases up from the regional offices to review them for legal
sufficiency and appropriateness of remedies. The Division of Elementary
and Secondary Education has three main areas of responsibility. The
first is to review cases that come out of the regions for policy
guidance, policy development, or analysis by the headquarters staff.
Second, it puts together policy manuals on issues such as bilingual
education, disciplinary matters, and age discrimination. Third, it is
responsible for the compliance requirements of the Emergency School Aid
Act.

The typical organization of a regional office is shown in Fig. 3.
The regional director usually has five divisions to administer. The
Program Review and Management Support (PRMS) division has the dual
function of providing management services for the office, such as hiring
and ordering office supplies, and serving as the control unit for
receiving communications to the office, including complaints. Both the
Elementary and Secondary and Post-secondary Education Divisions are
staffed by equal opportunity specialists (EOSs) who serve as the primary
point of contact between recipients and OCR. The attorneys units are a
fairly recent addition to OCR. They vary across the country in staff
size from 2 to 14. They are responsible for ensuring that OCR conducts

_____

[1] The last of these is not discussed here because it is not
germane to this report.

- 113 -

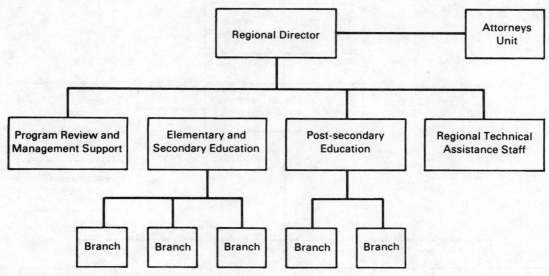

NOTE: Investigators are located in branches.

Fig. 3 -- Typical OCR regional office structure

legally sufficient investigations and produces findings that are legally satisfactory. An even newer addition to the regional offices is the Regional Technical Assistance Staff (RTAS), who provide services and information to recipients affected by Section 504.

OFFICE OF SPECIAL EDUCATION

Unlike OCR, which is geographically dispersed, OSE is found only in Washington, D.C. Its structure is presented in Fig. 4.

The Division of Innovation and Development is responsible for administering discretionary model programs, research grants, and support for services to deaf-blind children. Within this Division are three branches. The Research Projects Branch sponsors research to improve educational opportunities for handicapped students and their teachers, including the development, validation, and testing of alternative educational programs, and the dissemination of reports and research findings. The Program Development Branch awards grants and contracts for early childhood education projects such as demonstration and outreach programs. It also supports elementary, secondary, and postsecondary education for the handicapped through Model Programs that

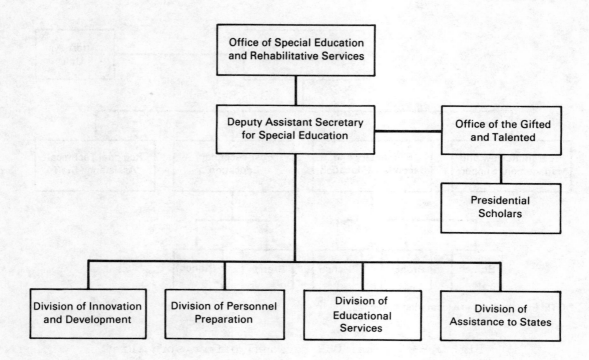

Fig. 4 -- Office of Special Education

demonstrate new or improved approaches and through vocational-technical programs to assist institutes of higher education. The State Implementation Branch focuses on programs for the severely handicapped and deaf-blind centers and services.

The Division of Personnel Preparation seeks to ensure an adequate supply of personnel able to meet the special education needs of the handicapped. Its current program has four emphases: (1) preparation of special educators; (2) preparation of support personnel; (3) training in special education for regular education teachers; and (4) development of instructional models. Most grant recipients are colleges and universities.

The Division of Educational Services provides services and technical assistance to strengthen the implementation of PL 94-142 through application of technological advancement, development and dissemination activities, and provision of educational resources. It has three branches. The Program Support Branch provides information and new educational advances by sponsoring analysis, development, and dissemination activities, including data on the oversight, administration, and implementation of federal laws for handicapped children. The Captioned Films and Media Applications Branch oversees the adaptation, production, and distribution of media, materials, and educational technology to expand and enrich educational and cultural opportunities for the handicapped. The Learning Resources Branch assists in and promotes the development of quality educational services to meet the requirements of PL 94-142. It award contracts for 13 Regional Resource Centers, which provide assistance to states, and 17 Direction Service Centers that provide assistance to parents.

Monitoring state administrative procedures is the responsibility of the Division of Assistance to States. That Division has three units. The development and dissemination of clarifications on past policies and the development of future policies for practices under PL 94-142 is the responsibility of the State Policy Development Branch. The receipt and processing of data on the number of beneficiaries (mandated by law to be conducted twice yearly by states), state plan approval, subsequent award of funds, and technical assistance are the responsibility of the Field Services Branch. The Compliance and Enforcement Branch develops and implements OSE's monitoring of state educational agencies. Although its activities have shifted over the past few years, the current direction of this Branch is to use data and information (in part provided by OCR) before visiting a state to construct a "state profile" for each SEA. The emphasis of the site visit is to review the states' own monitoring functions; the state profile is used to target specific problem areas for scrutiny (e.g., least restrictive environment and child-find efforts).